SCANDIKITCHEN
Christmas

SCANDIKITCHEN
Christmas

recipes and traditions from Scandinavia

BRONTË AURELL
Photography by Peter Cassidy

RYLAND PETERS & SMALL
LONDON • NEW YORK

Dedication
Til Mor og Far

Senior Designer
Sonya Nathoo

Senior Editor
Gillian Haslam

Head of Production
Patricia Harrington

Art Director
Leslie Harrington

Editorial Director
Julia Charles

Publisher
Cindy Richards

Food Stylist
Kathy Kordalis

Prop Stylist
Tony Hutchinson

Indexer
Hilary Bird

First published in 2018 by
Ryland Peters & Small
20–21 Jockey's Fields
London WC1R 4BW
and
Ryland Peters & Small
341 E 116th St
New York NY 10029
www.rylandpeters.com

Text © Brontë Aurell 2018

Design and commissioned photographs
© Ryland Peters & Small 2018

ISBN: 978-1-78879-025-3

10 9 8 7 6 5

Printed and bound in China.

CIP data from the Library of Congress
has been applied for.
A CIP record for this book is available
from the British Library.

Notes for cooks
* Both British (metric) and American
(imperial plus US cups) are included
in these recipes; however, it is important
to work with one set of measurements
and not alternate between the two
within a recipe.
* All butter is salted unless specified
otherwise.
* All eggs are medium (UK) or large
(US), unless specified as large, in which
case US extra large should be used.
Uncooked or partially cooked eggs should
not be served to the very old, frail, young
children, pregnant women or those with
compromised immune systems.
* Ovens should be preheated to the
specified temperatures. We recommend
using an oven thermometer. If using a
fan-assisted oven, adjust temperatures
according to the manufacturer's
instructions.
* When a recipe calls for the grated zest
of citrus fruit, buy unwaxed fruit and wash
well before using. If you can only find
treated fruit, scrub well in warm soapy
water before using.

Author's credits
The author would like to thank neighbours Mac & Wild/
Ardgay Game Inverness for supplying the best venison,
The Swedish Church in London for the Dala horse, and Jon
Anders Fjelsrud for help with aquavit cocktails.

Photography credits
All photography by Peter Cassidy except: p28 left Merethe
Svarstad Eeg/EyeEm/Getty Images, p28 right Johner
Images/Getty Images, p29 left Jo Tyler/Ryland Peters &
Small, p29 centre AnjelikaGretskaia/Getty Images, p29 right
Johner Images/Getty Images, p76 left Torbjorn Arvidson/
Getty Images, p76 centre Johner Images/Getty Images,
p77 right Johner Images/Getty Images, p100 left Cultura RF/
Christoffer Askman/Getty Images, p100 right Johner
Images/Getty Images.

CONTENTS

INTRODUCTION

The first Christmas at ScandiKitchen, over a decade ago, was a revelation to my husband Jonas and I. We didn't quite appreciate what it meant to run a café and shop that could provide all the foods that our fellow Scandinavians in London were missing. The emotional impact it had on our customers was overwhelming. To have people standing in our little shop with tears in their eyes because they couldn't make it back home and to help them enjoy their foods and traditions was a humbling experience then, and every Christmas since. No matter where you're from, when the call of home pulls at your heartstrings, only something genuine can help to relieve the ache. Food reconnects us in the form of scents, tastes and deep memories of years gone by. In one bite, you're back home – even if only for a brief moment.

To help a Norwegian recreate the cookies her grandmother used to make, to give a Dane the right sort of cherry sauce, to present a Swede with a bottle of glögg – Jonas and I feel so privileged to help Scandinavian families far away from home and to teach people how to incorporate new foods into their own Christmas meal, and over the years I've written down numerous instructions for cooking our festive dishes.

By the First Sunday of Advent we're ready not only to provide relief from homesickness, but also to teach anyone who will listen about the joy we Scandinavians find in Christmas. It may be dark and bitterly cold outside, but our hearts are some of the warmest you'll ever find. Our homes are lit by candles, we offer home-baked goods and spiced wines to everyone, and we let people into our usually reserved personal worlds. Everything in Scandinavia starts to smell of cinnamon and ginger, and we long for any sign of snowflakes to make us huddle up even more in our cocoons of Christmas *hygge*. Scandinavians embrace this season with such authenticity that I think people from elsewhere find it hard not to be swept along.

Scandinavia is so very big, and our food culture varied, so there are aspects I simply couldn't include in this book or it would stretch to several volumes. I have tried to balance tradition with a few new things, and hope you find inspiration to create a taste of Scandinavian Christmas.

This book was written by candlelight in my warm kitchen, with a never-ending scent of spice and festive music playing in the background, and the recipes were all tasted by the people I love. This is the book I hope my daughters will one day give to their grandchildren to show them how we did Christmas when they were Scandinavian kids growing up in London.

God jul, Brontë x

THE SCANDI CHRISTMAS PANTRY

'What can I use instead of...' is probably the most common question I'm asked when it comes to Scandinavian recipes. 'What is this spice called in English' is the second (I'm also asked to translate from English to Scandinavian languages for plenty of homesick Scandis, too). Sometimes the answers are not that simple, so here are some of the most common ingredients we use for Yuletide cooking, along with their names in Danish, Swedish and Norwegian.

BERRIES
Cloudberry
Multebær (D), Hjortron (S), Multe (N)
These orange berries, which look a bit like plump raspberries except for the colour, are found in the wild and are almost impossible to cultivate artificially. They can't be picked by machine, only by hand, and even that is tricky as the berries burst easily. Cloudberry season is around three weeks long, so that only adds to the cost and scarcity of the fruit. Frozen cloudberries are much easier to get hold of than fresh, but they are still expensive. Most Scandinavian shops stock cloudberry jam/preserves, which can be substituted for fresh berries in almost every recipe. In North America, cloudberries are often referred to as 'bakeapples'.

The cloudberry is very tart and pairs very well with apples, strong cheeses and vanilla (the jam is particularly wonderful heated up and poured over vanilla ice cream). To replace this flavour in recipes is hard, and a tart raspberry is the closest ingredient in taste.

Lingonberry
Tyttebær (D, N), Lingon (S)
Northern Scandinavians have lingonberries in their freezers throughout the year, while fresh ones are picked in August. The berry is small, red and tart, and found in abundance in Sweden, Norway and Finland. From the same family as the cranberry, the tartness of a lingonberry lends itself well to being served with meat (it is most famously served with meatballs). Lingonberries can also be used in cookies and cakes – pair them with something quite sweet, as they are really quite sharp in flavour. If you can't get hold of lingonberries, substitute with raspberries for sweet recipes, or cranberries for savoury dishes.

Sea buckthorn
Havtorn (D, S), Tindved (N)
Sea buckthorn grows wild across Scandinavia, parts of the UK, parts of Canada and as far east as China. It is quite unpleasant to eat raw, and some people find the smell of the fresh juice offensive! However, when sugar is added, the flavour complexities change. It is brilliant in jam and desserts. It's also good for you, being rich in vitamin C and carotenoids.

HERBS & SPICES
Caraway
Kommen (D), Kummin (S), Karve (N)
In Denmark and Sweden, the word for caraway sounds similar to cumin, so it is often translated incorrectly in recipes (cumin itself is *spidskommen* or *spiskummin*). We use caraway seeds a lot in breads, as well as cheeses.

Cardamom
Kardemomme (D, N), Kardemumma (S)
It's said that the Vikings first brought this spice back from Constantinople (now known as

Istanbul), but there is little to support this idea. However, around 1300, a Danish monk used cardamom in a cookbook influenced by Moorish recipes (*Libellus de arte coquinaria*), which is the earliest evidence we have for the spice's appearance in Scandinavian cooking. Today, we use cardamom a lot, including in the dough for our renowned cinnamon buns. I always buy the little seeds and crush them in a spice grinder for maximum flavour – it beats the pre-ground variety hands down, and really lifts the flavour of the buns.

Cinnamon
Kanel (D, S, N)
Some cheaper varieties of cinnamon are made from cassia bark, which contains high levels of coumarin (not good for you in high doses). If you can, go for high-grade Ceylon cinnamon instead, which has lower levels of coumarin and a better flavour.

Cloves
Nellike (D), Nejlika (S), Nellik (N)
Cloves are used whole in aquavit and mulled wine, and sometimes on Swedish Christmas ham. Crushed cloves are common in biscuits and cookies. In Denmark at Christmas-time, windows are often decorated with fresh oranges studded with whole cloves – a great way to bring a wonderfully festive scent into your house! The word *krydd* (spice) sometimes prefixes the word for clove in all three languages.

Dill
Dild (D), Dill (S, N)
We use dill a lot to give a lift to salads, fish or chicken. Crown dill (where the herb has been allowed to flower) is used for its strong flavour at crayfish parties. That variety is quite hard to get hold of outside Sweden, but you can always grow your own or use fresh dill instead.

Fennel seed
Fennikelfrø (D, N), Fänkålsfrö (S)
We use fennel seed mainly in bread, both for loaves and as a flavouring for crispbread.

Ginger
Ingefær (D, N), Ingefära (S)
Ground ginger is commonly used in biscuits, cookies and cakes. Whole dried ginger is essential in mulled wine, but fresh ginger is actually not that common in Scandinavia.

Saffron
Safran (D, N), Saffran (S)
Like cardamom, the origins of saffron's arrival into Scandinavia are unclear. Some say it came via ancient Asian trading routes, while others think it was brought northwards from France and Italy. Regardless, saffron in Scandinavia has always been used for special occasions only, most likely because of its high value (if you're shopping for it in Scandinavia, it's probably kept behind the shop counter or till). However, it is an essential ingredient at Christmas time for Lucia buns. We commonly use ground saffron, but if you are using strands, grind them well first. To intensify the colour, soak the strands in warm water before using.

Salt
Salt (D, S, N)
Scandinavians have been preserving food in salt for centuries, so it's not surprising that we have a love for using it in anything from well-seasoned savoury dishes to sprinkling it on biscuits or cakes. Not all salt is equal, but if you ever spot a brand called North Sea Salt Works, buy it.

Seville orange peel
Pomeransskal (D, S), Pomeransskall (N)
We use this in mulled wine and also in some Christmas breads and biscuits. You can substitute with normal dried bitter orange peel, but the flavour will not be as subtle.

Vanilla
Vanille (D), Vanilj (S), Vanilje (N)
Most Scandinavian cookbooks use vanilla sugar in recipes, which is a quick and easy substitute for whole vanilla pods/beans. You can buy this in Scandinavian food shops, or make your own by grinding 275 g/2 cups icing/confectioners' sugar with 2 dried vanilla pods/beans in a food processor or spice grinder until pulverized. Sift to remove the woody bits and use as needed. You can normally just substitute with vanilla extract or vanilla pods/beans too. If you are buying, Tørsleffs is a great brand.

OILS, VINEGARS & MUSTARDS
24% spirit vinegar
Eddike (D), Ättika/Ättiksprit (S), Eddik (N)
This is very strong pickling vinegar and needs to be diluted to the strength specified in your recipe – usually 5–6% for vegetables, 12% for herring or other cured fish. You can buy this vinegar in Scandinavian and Chinese supermarkets.

Mustard
Sennep (D, N), Senap (S)
Scandinavians favour sweet, strong mustards. You can substitute a grainy Dijon, but in some recipes you may need to add a pinch of sugar as our mustards – even strong ones – also tend to be quite sweet. For Swedish Christmas recipes, quite often a regional mustard from the southern region of Skåne is used (*skånsk senap*). If you cannot get it, add a little sugar to Dijon mustard.

Rapeseed/canola oil
Rapsolie (D), Rapsolja (S), Rapsolje (N)
Healthy rapeseed/canola oil is popular all over Scandinavia. However, not all rapeseed oils are the same, and an inferior one won't do your dish any favours, so always use the best quality.

YEAST AND LEAVENERS
Baker's ammonia/hartshorn
Hjortetaksalt (D), Hjorthornssalt (S), Hornsalt (N)
Used in old recipes to ensure cookies rise and get crispy at low temperatures, baker's ammonia gives off a strong smell during baking, but this disappears as the biscuits cool. I have not used it in this book, but you can buy it online or at some pharmacies, as well as in many Scandi food shops. Traditionally made from the ground antlers of young stags, these days it's all chemical. When using baker's ammonia, don't eat the raw dough. Substitute with baking powder, but the result will not be as crispy.

Fresh yeast
Gær (D), Jäst (S), Gjær (N)
I always use fresh yeast, but 25 g/$7/8$ oz. fresh, compressed yeast is equivalent to 13 g/$1/2$ oz. active dry yeast granules (activate them for 15 minutes before adding the other ingredients). Instant dried yeast sachets are also an option – follow the guidelines for the dosage, and always add to the dry ingredients, not the wet ones. Liquid hotter than 36–37°C/96–98°F will kill fresh yeast, as will salt added directly to it. Fresh yeast can be frozen, but it will turn to liquid when defrosted, so pack it in little bags.

Potassium carbonate/potash
Potaske (D), Kaliumkarbonat (S, N)
Many old Danish and German recipes call for the use of potash, which is quite a strong chemical

used to obtain a very crispy finish on biscuits and cookies. While I agree that it makes for super crispy results, I do think bicarbonate of/baking soda can be used instead, as long as there is some liquid in the recipe (if not, use baking powder). If you do use potash, make sure it is of food grade and diluted to liquid before added. I don't use it in this book.

FLOURS & GRAINS

Light rye flour, type 997

This is a sifted rye from Germany – not as white as white rye, which has been sifted twice. I love baking with this flour, but it is usually only available online (in the UK, try Shipton Mills).

Malt

Malt (D, S, N)

You can buy barley malt protein powder or syrup online. We also sometimes use a low-alcohol malt beer in rye bread dough. If you cannot get malt, use normal dark syrup for rye bread instead.

Oats

Havre (D, S, N)

Used in porridge, granola, muesli and baking. We also eat raw oats with milk for breakfast. Oat flakes (jumbo oats) or cut oats are favoured, and we don't really use oatmeal.

Potato flour

Kartoffelmel (D), Potatismjöl (S), Potetmel (N)

Some recipes call for potato flour to thicken a sauce or a dish. You can buy it in speciality food stores, especially Scandinavian, Italian and Polish. Once potato starch is added, the dish should not be allowed to boil (especially in fruit-based sauces, as these will go cloudy after boiling). You can substitute with cornflour/cornstarch, but if you need a less cloudy result, arrowroot is the best thing to use.

Rye flakes

Rugflager (D), Rågflingor (S), Rugflak (N)

I love using rye flakes in granola, flapjacks and porridge (mixed with normal oats) for their nutty flavour and a good bite. Available in health-food stores, they take longer to cook and are quite chewy. If you are using oats in a recipe, consider mixing 80% oats and 20% rye.

Rye flour

Rugmel (D, N), Rågmjöl (S)

You can't work your way through Scandinavian food without encountering rye flour. Wholegrain rye is common in supermarkets – it's very strong and hearty, and is great for baking dark rye breads. Wheat flour cannot just be replaced with wholegrain rye, though – it has less gluten than wheat, and it does not stretch the same way. You can experiment with replacing 10% of the white flour with rye, then increase the amount a little more the next time.

Rye flour mix

Rugsigtemel (D), Rågsikt (S), Siktet rugmel (N)

In Sweden and Denmark, rye flour mixes are very common. They're usually 60% white wheat flour and 40% light rye (type 997), sifted together. Make this at home by mixing the same quantities.

Rye kernels

Rugkerner (D), Rågkärnor (S), Rugkjerner (N)

There are two kinds on the market – the whole rye kernel and the kibbled or cut one. You need the whole one if boiling to include in salads or other dishes, while the kibbled variety is essential when making good rye bread, where the whole one would be too hard to use. If you can only get the whole variety, you can chop the rye kernels in a food processor with a few quick pulses (not too much – you only just want to cut them in half).

Spelt flour
Speltmel (D, N), Dinkelmjöl/Speltvetemjöl (S)
This is an older type of wheat grain, and less refined. You can get both white and wholegrain spelt flour, which contain less gluten than other wheat flours.

White rye flour
Hvid rugmel (D), Vitt rågmjöl (S), Hvit rugmel (N)
In this book I have used a lot of white rye. It is now widely available and I find it nice to bake with. While wholegrain rye can sometimes be a bit harsh, white rye is a great way to still use rye instead of wheat. It still needs some wheat for the gluten to stretch when baking bread, though. In essence, the rye has been sifted and the husk has been removed. This also means fewer health benefits, but I do think the taste of rye remains.

OTHER
Aquavit
Aquavit (D), Akvavit (S), Akevitt (N)
A grain-based spirit flavoured with herbs and strong spices (such as fennel, aniseed and caraway), aquavit can have many different flavours and types, so there's so much scope for development and experimentation (such as in cocktails). Most people often enjoy it as part of a smörgåsbord or with pickled herring.

You can get young aquavits (almost always clear) or aged ones (which look similar to whisky). Despite what trendy bars might say, not all aquavits can be enjoyed at their best when served ice-cold, so check to see what the brand advises. There are many types of aquavit which, like whisky, are made in different ways to affect the taste. Aged aquavits, such as Aalborg Nordguld, OP Anderson, or Linie, have more rounded flavours and colours.

Making a flavoured aquavit-style drink at home is not difficult, but I do recommend you get a base aquavit such as Brøndums Snaps Klar or Aalborg Basis, developed specifically for adding your own flavours. Vodka can also be used. The main thing to remember when making an aquavit is that fresh flavourings such as dill or other herbs only need a few days in the alcohol, while hard spices such as cinnamon or liquorice root may require a few weeks.

Buttermilk
Kærnemælk (D), Kärnmjölk (S), Kjernemelk (N)
Buttermilk often makes an appearance in Danish cuisine. I like using it in batters for pancakes and in cakes, and it also works well in other types of baking. If you can't get buttermilk, use whole milk with a few drops of lemon juice added and left for 15 minutes before using. It's not quite the same, but it is a fair substitute if needs must.

Marzipan
Marcipan (D), Marsipan (S, N)
Not all marzipans are the same. High-quality marzipan with a minimum of 60% almonds is usually only available in speciality stores, and can be quite pricy owing to the sheer amount of almonds used. If you can only get a marzipan with around 50% almonds, that will usually be OK, but will be a little harder to work with due to the extra sugar content.

Viennese nougat
Wiener nougat (D), Wienernougat (S, N)
A hazelnut praline paste mixed with tempered chocolate. Sometimes it is sold as a spread, but you need to get the block version for recipes in this book. You can make it at home, but it's hard to get the same smooth texture as shop-bought. Danish brand Odense does a really good 250-g/9-oz. block, if you can get it.

ADVENT GATHERINGS

Weekends in December are for visiting friends, family and neighbours. It's the time to catch up and reconnect – and for drinking lots of warming glögg. It's for celebrating St Lucia and the hope of lighter days ahead, and making sure you light a candle every Sunday. When that First Sunday of Advent comes along, we allow ourselves to really start preparing for the big day.

scones med västerbottensost

MINI SCONES WITH VÄSTERBOTTEN CHEESE

I often serve these mini scones as filling canapés. You can also make these as regular-sized cheese scones by simply choosing a larger cutter and amending the baking time accordingly. Serve as they are, or split them open and fill with crème fraîche or sour cream mixed with chopped chives, or even top with a dollop of thick crème fraîche and red lumpfish roe. They also work well with a sliver of salmon.

250g/2 cups plain/all-purpose flour

1 tablespoon baking powder

a pinch of paprika

$\frac{1}{2}$ teaspoon salt

freshly ground black pepper

75 g/$\frac{1}{3}$ cup cold butter, cut into cubes

150 g/5$\frac{1}{2}$ oz. Västerbotten cheese (or other hard cheese, such as pecorino), finely grated (divide into one pile of 100 g/3$\frac{1}{2}$ oz., and another of 50 g/2 oz.)

125 ml/$\frac{1}{2}$ cup cold milk

50 g/$\frac{1}{2}$ cup finely chopped, toasted walnuts (optional)

beaten egg or milk, for brushing

MAKES ABOUT 40 MINI SCONES

Preheat the oven to 200°C (400°F) Gas 6.

Put the flour, baking power, paprika, salt and pepper into a bowl, then add the cold, cubed butter. Rub until the mixture resembles a crumble. Add the larger quantity of cheese and mix, then gradually add the milk to form a dough. Try not to overwork it – less is more, it simply needs to be evenly together. The more you work the dough, the denser your scones will be. Mix in the chopped walnuts, if using.

Very gently roll out the dough to a thickness of around 1.5 cm/$\frac{5}{8}$ in. Gently brush with a little beaten egg or milk, then scatter over the remaining cheese and press down slightly. Using a 3-cm/1$\frac{1}{4}$-in. cookie cutter, punch out your scones (don't twist them out). You can gently re-roll the remaining dough to use it all up.

Place on a baking sheet and bake in the preheated oven for around 8–9 minutes until browned, risen and baked through.

ädelost och pepparkakor
BLUE CHEESE & GINGER STICKS

When I was first offered *pepparkakor* on a cheese board in Sweden, I did find it a little peculiar. However, it's a truly wonderful combination. You can use shop-bought ginger thins for this, but I like to make mine using the *pepparkaka* dough in this book (see page 56) and shaping them into long breadsticks. I serve the sticks in a jar with the bowl of dip next to it.

This dip is also a great side to serve at an Advent party or for Christmas nibbles. The *pepparkakor* really work with a lot of different cheeses, so make them a regular accompaniment to your cheeseboard.

200 g/7 oz. blue cheese, crumbled (I like to use Blå Kornblomst, but St Agur or Stilton also work well)

200 g/1 cup crème fraîche or sour cream

100 g/½ cup natural yogurt

a few drops of white wine vinegar

salt and freshly ground black pepper

SERVES 5–6, AS PART OF A LARGER SNACK TABLE

Mix the blue cheese, crème fraîche or sour cream, yogurt and white wine vinegar together, and add seasoning to taste. If it is too hard to dip, add more crème fraîche, or even a dash of milk (depending on the cheese you decide to use, the texture can be different) – you need a mixture that's easy to dip.

Chill in the fridge before serving.

Ginger sticks
Roll out the gingerbread dough (see page 56) and slice into sticks. Place on a baking sheet and bake in an oven preheated to 200°C (400°F) Gas 6 for 7–8 minutes, until slightly browned around the edges. Allow to cool on a wire rack.

æbleskiver

DANISH PANCAKE BALLS

In Denmark, Christmas will never be Christmas without these little pancake balls. The word *æbleskiver* literally means 'apple slices', because in the 1700s these were actually slices of apple, dipped in batter and fried. Nowadays, people rarely use apple – the balls are usually cooked, dusted with sugar, dipped in raspberry jam and eaten. That said, I think that apples give these a bit of a lift. If you prefer them plain, simply leave out the filling. These are also found in southern Norway, where they are known as *munker*. You will need to use an *æbleskiver* pan – a round pan with indentations in the surface. They are quite easy to buy online.

3 eggs, separated
300 ml/1¼ cups buttermilk
100 ml/⅓ cup double/heavy cream
1 tablespoon caster/superfine sugar
½ teaspoon salt
1 teaspoon baking powder
½ teaspoon bicarbonate of/baking soda
1 teaspoon ground cardamom
200 g/1½ cups plain/all-purpose flour
1 teaspoon vanilla extract
50 g/3½ tablespoons melted butter, for cooking
icing/confectioners' sugar and raspberry jam/preserves, to serve

FILLING (OPTIONAL)
2 apples, peeled, cored and chopped into small pieces
25 g/1¾ tablespoons butter
2 teaspoons ground cinnamon
50 g/¼ cup sugar
1 tablespoon vanilla extract

æbleskiver pan

MAKES AROUND 30

Mix the egg yolks, buttermilk and cream in a bowl.

In another bowl, mix together the dry ingredients – the sugar, salt, baking powder, bicarbonate of/baking soda, cardamom and flour, as well as the vanilla extract.

In a third bowl, whisk the egg whites on high speed until stiff.

Mix together the wet and dry ingredients, then carefully fold in the whisked egg whites. Leave to rest for 30 minutes in the fridge.

If including the filling, place the ingredients in a saucepan, bring to the boil, then leave to simmer until the apple goes soft.

When you're ready to cook the balls, preheat the *æbleskiver* pan over a high heat, then reduce the heat to medium and add a bit of melted butter to each hole. Carefully add enough batter to each hole so that it reaches about 2.5 mm/⅛ in. from the top. Add 1 teaspoon of filling mixture to the middle of each hole, if including it. Leave to cook for a few minutes, then, using a knitting needle or chopstick, carefully turn the balls over to cook on the other side. If you have filled the holes too much, this can be tricky, but you'll get the hang of it.

Once browned on all sides (this will take about 3–4 minutes per batch), keep the cooked *æbleskiver* in a warm oven until you are done – this will also help to cook them through.

Serve dusted with icing/confectioners' sugar and a little pot of raspberry jam/preserves for dipping.

laksepaté
SALMON & PRAWN TERRINE

This is a tasty dish that can be made the day before and arranged straight from the fridge just before serving. It's not quite a pâté and not quite a terrine, but it's lovely eaten with crispbread or rye bread.

1 small shallot, peeled

300 g/10¹/2 oz. raw salmon fillets, skin removed

200 g/7 oz. raw prawns/shrimp, peeled, plus extra to garnish

150 ml/²/3 cup double/heavy cream

1 egg

1 tablespoon cornflour/cornstarch

freshly grated zest and juice of ¹/4 lemon

20 g/1 oz. dill, leaves chopped (plus some sprigs to garnish)

ROE DRESSING

50 g/1³/4 oz. red lumpfish roe

150 ml/²/3 cup crème fraîche or sour cream

salt and freshly ground black pepper

SERVES 6–8 AS PART OF A SMÖRGÅSBORD

SALMON TERRINE CANAPÉS

3 slices of rye bread, buttered

slices of Salmon and Prawn Terrine (see above)

2–3 avocados (not too overripe, but easily sliceable)

freshly squeezed lemon juice

3 tablespoons crème fraîche or sour cream

2¹/2 teaspoons red lumpfish roe

sprigs of fresh dill

MAKES APPROX. 10 CANAPÉS

Preheat the oven to 160°C (325°F) Gas 3. Line a small, deep terrine or baking dish (500–600-ml/17–20-oz. volume) with baking parchment. Take an oven dish or baking tray into which your terrine will fit easily, fill halfway with water, and place the dish of water in the oven.

Chop the shallot in a food processor, then add the salmon and prawns/shrimp, and pulse a few times until broken up but still containing large chunks. Add the remaining ingredients except for the dill and pulse again briefly, taking care not to make it too smooth. Finally, fold in the dill. Place the mixture in the lined terrine. Cover the top with a sheet of baking parchment and pat it down a bit.

Place the dish inside the larger oven dish or tray of heated water and bake for 45 minutes until just set. It should have a slight wobble, and the cooking time will vary depending the depth of your dish. Check it after 20 minutes if using a fairly shallow oven dish.

Remove the terrine from the oven, allow to cool, then chill in the fridge overnight.

For the dressing, combine the ingredients, season, and set aside.

To serve whole, turn the terrine out onto a serving dish and garnish with a few more prawns/shrimp and sprigs of dill. Serve with the roe dressing on the side.

Variations
To serve as canapés, cut the bread into pieces around 3 x 2 cm/1¹/4 x ³/4 in. Using a very sharp knife, cut the terrine into similar-sized pieces and place on top of the bread. Peel the avocados and slice very finely, then place on the terrine. Squeeze over the lemon juice (to prevent the avocado going brown). Pipe a blob of crème fraîche on top, then add ¹/4 teaspoon roe, a fresh sprig of dill and a grinding of black pepper.

If you are not keen on roe dressing, mix together 100 ml/¹/3 cup crème fraîche or sour cream, 100 ml/¹/3 cup plain skyr (or similar), 3–4 tablespoons finely chopped chives, 1 tablespoon chopped dill, squeeze of fresh lemon juice and salt and freshly ground black pepper in a bowl and chill until ready to serve.

FOUR OPEN-SANDWICH CANAPÉS

Canapés are fiddly things, and they require attention and time to look nice. Still, I think it's worth preparing a few when inviting people over. Use these recipes as a guide – I have left them deliberately vague in parts, because most can be amended to fit what you have available, as long as the ingredients go together.

If you change the size and shape, always bear in mind that canapés should be eaten in one or two bites – never more, or it becomes messy. If in doubt, smaller is usually better. You will need a piping/pastry bag and nozzle/tip.

aeg og dild
EGG & DILL

3 hard-boiled/cooked eggs, finely chopped

3 tablespoons crème fraîche or sour cream, plus extra for piping

1 tablespoon mayonnaise

3 tablespoons finely chopped chives

2 tablespoons finely chopped dill

$1/2$ teaspoon Dijon mustard

3 slices of rye bread, buttered

salt and freshly ground black pepper

MAKES APPROX.
10 CANAPÉS

Mix the egg and other topping ingredients together until combined, then chill.

Using a 2.5-cm/1-in. cookie cutter with high sides, cut one circle from the bread, but do not remove the bread from the cutter. Fill the hole with $1\frac{1}{2}$ teaspoons of the egg mixture and press it down gently. Press out the canapé from the bread side, out of the top end, and place on the serving platter. Repeat.

Serve topped with a dollop of crème fraîche or sour cream and more herbs.

skagenröra
TOAST SKAGEN

sourdough bread

1–2 tablespoons mayonnaise

25–35 fresh prawns/shrimp, cooked

2–3 teaspoons crème fraîche or sour cream

lemon zest

horseradish sauce (optional)

$2\frac{1}{2}$ teaspoons red lumpfish roe

freshly chopped dill or chives

salt and freshly ground black pepper

MAKES APPROX.
10 CANAPÉS

Toast several slices of good-quality sourdough bread and leave to cool. Press out 10 rounds using a cookie cutter 2.5 cm/1 in. in diameter.

Put the mayonnaise in a piping/pastry bag and add a small dollop to each round, then place the prawns/shrimps on neatly to cover. Add a dollop of crème fraîche or sour cream seasoned with salt, pepper and lemon zest (and a bit of horseradish, if you have it).

Add $1/4$ teaspoon of roe, and either dill or chives to garnish, plus an extra twirl of lemon zest.

roget laks
SMOKED SALMON

200 g/7 oz. smoked salmon, thinly sliced

100 g/½ cup cream cheese, plus extra to serve

finely chopped chives

2–3 slices of rye bread, buttered

cucumber, shaved

grated lemon zest and freshly squeezed lemon juice

micro herbs

salt and freshly ground black pepper

MAKES APPROX. 10 CANAPÉS

Place a piece of clingfilm/plastic wrap on the work surface and carefully lay the salmon out so it just overlaps and you get a piece approx. 30 x 5 cm/12 x 2 in. (you can also make two pieces if easier). Place the cream cheese in a piping/pastry bag and pipe down the length of the salmon slightly towards one side, then add salt, pepper and a sprinkling of very finely chopped chives.

Using the clingfilm/plastic wrap to guide you, roll the salmon around the cheese so you end up with a long log. Tighten the clingfilm and place in the fridge for a few hours to firm up a little.

Cut the rye bread into 3 x 1.5-cm/1¼ x ⅝-in. pieces. Using a very sharp knife, cut the salmon roll into 3-cm/1¼-in. long pieces, removing the clingfilm/plastic wrap afterwards.

Place folded cucumber shavings on each piece of bread, using a little more cream cheese to help keep them in place. Place a salmon roll on each piece of bread, then pipe 2–3 dots of cream cheese on the top of each one. Drizzle with a little lemon juice and add micro herbs and maybe some lemon zest on top.

roast beef
RARE ROAST BEEF

3 slices of rye bread, buttered

150 g/5 oz. rare roast beef, very finely sliced

20 small shallot rings

oil, for frying (optional)

plain/all-purpose flour, for dusting (optional)

3–4 tablespoons Danish remoulade

sprigs of fresh chervil, to garnish

salt and freshly ground black pepper

MAKES APPROX. 10 CANAPÉS

Cut the buttered rye bread into squares of around 2.5 cm/1 in. Place a slice of beef on each square, making sure it is arranged to give the canapé some height (this can take a little practice – don't make it look too uniform).

You can use the shallot rings raw, or if you prefer them crispy, dust them with flour, then fry in hot oil until brown. Drain on paper towels, and leave to crisp up.

Put the Danish remoulade into a piping/pastry bag, then pipe a little hazelnut-sized blob of Danish remoulade on each slice of beef. Add the shallot rings and garnish with sprigs of chervil. Season with salt and pepper.

Note that Danish remoulade is not the same as the French variety. You can find it in Scandinavian shops and online.

Advent in Scandinavia

Considering how much Scandinavians tend to long for Christmas, we don't actually start celebrating that early. Here in London, you can buy baubles in summer, and by early autumn, shop windows are full of stuff necessary for the 'perfect Christmas'.

However, in Scandinavia, the build-up is far less obvious and, I believe, less commercial, perhaps because the unspoken rule is that Christmas starts on the First Sunday of Advent – and absolutely not before. The Christian tradition of marking the four Sundays before Christmas is an old one, but Scandinavians have celebrated the winter solstice for even longer.

One reason why candles in the dark have such significance for us is the anticipation of lighter days ahead. Our winters are shrouded in so much darkness, so any speck of light helps us to look forward. On each Sunday of Advent, a candle is lit on an Advent wreath, celebrating another step closer to Christmas.

Every Sunday in December is reserved for visits with family and friends. We heat up the glögg (see pages 32–33) and open our doors to welcome visitors, who will also be offered ginger biscuits and other baked goods. Sometimes several visits are made in one day, so glögg is usually offered in modest servings: drink too much of the good stuff and your nose and ears will go red, and you'll look like a Christmas elf.

One of the biggest celebrations in December is the feast of St Lucia on 13th December, always celebrated in the early morning on the day, but also on the closest Sunday. Lucia celebrations have strong Christian and pagan roots, like so

many Scandinavian traditions, including Yule itself. This day celebrates St Lucia of Syracuse in Sicily, whose feast coincided with the winter solstice until calendar reforms, and represents the arrival of light into the darkness. Lucia's name is similar to our words for 'light'.

Lucia night is also known as *Lussenatt* – the night of Lusse. On this night – the longest night of the year – it was said that the animals could talk. Evil spirits would roam the earth, and all slaughter and preparation for solstice celebrations would have to be completed before this night.

Across towns, schools and places of work, long processions take place with people dressed in white robes, singing traditional carols. These start early, to break the long darkness and to sing in the light once again. The singers wear

red sashes around their waists to symbolize martyrdom and carry a candle in their hands while they sing. At the front of the procession is a young girl leading the Lucia train, wearing a crown of real candles in her hair. She is the Lucia Bride. We sing in the light, celebrating that the darkness is now behind us and we can look forward to the lighter days.

On Lucia day in Denmark, everybody eats the little pancake dumplings called *æbleskiver* (see page 20). In Sweden and Norway, more traditional saffron buns known as *lussebullar* or *lussekatter* are enjoyed (see page 30).

In Sweden, these traditions are particularly strong, and it is quite likely that if you know any Swedes or happen to be in Sweden on this day, you'll end up taking part in the celebrations, too. There is absolutely no better way to get me into the spirit of Christmas than by listening to the main St Lucia song performed by candlelight, as I shelter from the cold with my family by my side.

lussebullar
LUCIA BUNS

Every Sunday in Advent is celebrated across Sweden, Norway and Denmark with glögg and, quite often, freshly baked Lucia buns. These traditional buns are always served on 13th December, when the arrival of Saint Lucia is celebrated. The buns are baked in an 'S' shape, with two raisins, one in each curve – another name for them is *lussekatter*, as they look a bit like the eyes of a cat (there's also a lot of cat-related superstition associated with these buns).

200 ml/^{3}/$_4$ cup whole milk

0.5 g (or the tiniest pinch) ground saffron

25 g/^{7}/$_8$ oz. fresh yeast

75 g/6 tablespoons caster/superfine sugar

100 ml/^{1}/$_3$ cup quark or Greek yogurt (or similar)

400–500 g/3–3^1/$_2$ cups strong bread flour, plus extra for dusting

^{1}/$_2$ teaspoon salt

100 g/7 tablespoons butter, softened and cubed

1 egg, beaten (reserve half for brushing)

a handful of raisins

pearl sugar (optional)

MAKES 16 BUNS

Heat the milk in a saucepan until finger-warm (no more than 37°C/98°F), then add the ground saffron.

In a stand mixer, add the fresh yeast and the milk-saffron mixture (again, no warmer than 37°C/98°F or the yeast will die). Mix for 1 minute, then add the sugar and stir until dissolved. Stir in the quark or yogurt until incorporated, then mix in about half the flour, as well as the salt. As you keep mixing, gradually add more flour, taking care not to add too much (saffron is very drying, so if you have a dry dough, the end result will also be dry). Add the butter and half of the egg and keep mixing, adding more flour as needed. This will take around 5 minutes.

When the dough is springy and well kneaded, leave to rest in a covered bowl in a warm place for about 40 minutes or until doubled in size.

Turn out the dough onto a floured surface and knead. Cut into 16 even pieces. Roll each piece into a roll 20 cm/8 in. long. Take each end and twist them back in on themselves in opposite directions so you end up with an S-shape. Line a baking tray with paper, then place each bun on it, ensuring there is good distance between each bun (or to shape into a wreath as in the photo, simply place the buns in a circle, leaving a 1-cm/^{1}/$_2$-in. gap between them as they spread during baking). Gently press a raisin into the centre of each swirl. Leave to rise for 20 minutes.

Preheat the oven to 170°C (340°F) Gas 3^1/$_2$.

Gently brush each bun with the remaining egg and bake in the preheated oven for 8–10 minutes, or until golden and done. Leave under a damp tea towel/dish towel for at least 10 minutes as soon as they come out of the oven to ensure no crust forms. If you wish, scatter over some pearl sugar.

Saffron dough dries out quickly, so either eat the buns on the day of baking or freeze as soon as they're cool. I also enjoy them slightly toasted when they're a few days old.

FOUR GLÖGGS

From the rich red wine glögg spiked with brandy or aquavit, to light or alcohol-free versions, every household in Scandinavia serves a version of mulled wine during the festive season. Visit any home during the cold days of December and you'll surely be offered a mug of this warm, comforting beverage. As with most mulled wines, glögg is meant to use up any wine you have left over. As you're adding sugar and heating, the wine's complexities are changed – so never use a vintage. Do, however, use good spices and experiment to make a glögg that works for you.

den bästa glöggen
ANNIKA'S GLÖGG

My Swedish sister-in-law Annika makes the best glögg in Scandinavia. This is a great one for all occasions and can be made ahead and kept in the bottle for quite a few weeks.

1 bottle of red wine (a cheap one will be fine)

2 cinnamon sticks

1 piece of dried ginger (5–6 g/$^1/4$ oz.)

1 piece of dried bitter Seville orange peel (5–6 g/$^1/4$ oz.)

8 whole green cardamom pods

15–16 whole cloves

80 g/6$^1/2$ tablespoons sugar

SERVES 3–4

Put all the ingredients into a large pan and heat to 80°C/176°F, taking care not to go above that to boiling point.

Turn off the heat and leave the wine to infuse for at least a couple of hours, then strain into a sealable bottle or a container you can cover.

To serve, reheat gently until hot.

hjortronglögg
ALCOHOL-FREE CLOUDBERRY GLÖGG

This works well with warm apple juice, and also with warm cider if you want a bit of alcohol but don't fancy a wine-based glögg.

100 ml/$^1/3$ cup apple juice

80 g/3 oz. frozen cloudberries

2 cinnamon sticks

$^1/4$ vanilla pod/bean

75 g/6 tablespoons sugar

5 whole green cardamom pods

TO SERVE

700 ml/3 cups apple juice

SERVES 3–4

Put all the ingredients in a pan with 100 ml/$^1/3$ cup water, bring to the boil and simmer for 10 minutes. Turn off the heat and leave to infuse for a few hours before straining into a sealable container or bottle. Make sure you mash the berries through a sieve/strainer to maximize their flavour. Store the extract in a sealed container in the fridge until you need it.

To serve, heat up the apple juice in a pan until it's hot, then add the extract to taste.

lingonglögg
LINGONBERRY GLÖGG

This glögg is fresher than the traditional red wine-only version – I love the tart notes of the berries. As with the cloudberry glögg, you're making a flavour extract to add to the wine before serving.

200 ml/³/₄ cup lingonberry cordial (or a similar, decent-quality berry cordial)

100 g/3¹/₂ oz. frozen lingonberries (or other berries)

50 g/¹/₄ cup sugar

2 cinnamon sticks

10 whole green cardamom pods

10 whole cloves

TO SERVE

1 bottle of red wine

lingonberries and raisins, to decorate

SERVES 3–4

Put all the ingredients in a pan with 100 ml/¹/₃ cup water and bring to the boil. Turn down the heat and leave to simmer for 10 minutes. Turn off the heat and leave to infuse for a few hours. Strain the liquid into a sealable container or bottle, mashing the berries through a sieve/strainer to get their juices out. Store the extract in the fridge until you need it.

To serve, heat the red wine until hot, but not boiling, and add the extract to taste. Add a few lingonberries to decorate, along with some raisins.

hvidvinsgløgg
WHITE-WINE GLØGG

As an alternative to traditional gløgg (as they call it in Denmark and Norway), white wine is lovely. It can often taste sour if reheated, so adding a flavour extract to the wine just before serving avoids this problem. Use a glögg extract within a few days of making it.

1 cinnamon stick

¹/₂ vanilla pod/bean

2–3 star anise

6 whole green cardamom pods

8 whole cloves

80 g/6¹/₂ tablespoons caster/superfine sugar

100 ml/¹/₃ cup apple juice

TO SERVE

1 bottle of white wine (a cheap one will be fine)

SERVES 3–4

Place all the ingredients in a pan and bring to the boil. Turn the heat down to low and leave to simmer for about 10 minutes. Turn off the heat, cover the pan and leave to cool for at least an hour (or overnight, if you can). Strain the extract into a sealable container or bottle to remove the spices and store in the fridge until you need it.

To serve, heat the white wine until hot but not boiling, then add the extract to taste.

Jons juleakvavit
JON'S CHRISTMAS AQUAVIT

No Christmas smörgåsbord is complete without a shot of aquavit. We usually drink it with pickled herring, as the sharp spirit complements the fish well. This Christmas aquavit recipe is inspired by glögg (see pages 32–33) and was created by Jon Anders Fjelsrud, an expert in aquavit and many other spirits, who hosts tastings in our café.

500 ml/2 cups vodka

1 tablespoon sugar

2 cinnamon sticks

10 g/¹/₃ oz. whole dried ginger

5–7g/¹/₄ oz. dried Seville orange peel (or other bitter orange peel)

20 whole green cardamom pods

20 whole cloves

1 tablespoon oak barrel smoking chips (optional – Jim Beam has its own brand of these for barbecuing, available online)

MAKES APPROX. 12 SHOTS

AQUAVIT BUBBLY

1 sugar cube, or same amount in sugar crystals

Angostura bitters

10–20 ml/2–4 teaspoons aged aquavit

Champagne, prosecco or cava

SERVES 1

Pour the vodka into a sealable container and add all the other ingredients. You'll need to leave it to infuse for weeks, so if you want this for Christmas, start in October.

Taste this every so often to see how the flavours are developing. You can add more vodka to dilute, or leave for longer to infuse if not strong enough. The aquavit is ready when you are.

Strain and serve chilled in shot glasses. Scandinavians have many songs to accompany the drinking of aquavit – see if you can manage to sing one!

Aquavit bubbly
This is a quick and easy way to Scandi-up your fizz with a Scandi twist. Use an aged aquavit with a golden colour (see page 12).

In each glass, place one sugar cube and add 2 drops of Angostura bitters. Add a small shot of aged aquavit and leave to dissolve. Start to pour over your bubbly and mix carefully (take care, it will fizz up). Gently continue to top up until the glass is full.

You can replace the sugar with cloudberries (or even cloudberry jam) and proceed as directed.

BISCUITS AND EDIBLE GIFTS

In Scandinavia, baking for the festive season starts early.
Old family recipes find their way back into kitchens, and
days are spent preparing treats for glögg parties and gifts
for friends. In my house, these days are also spent making
Christmas decorations with the kids and really getting into
the mood (mum-dancing is allowed: it's my kitchen).

serinakaker

NORWEGIAN BUTTER COOKIES

These traditional butter cookies are served at Christmas time in Norway. They are quick to make and taste delicious. If you can't get hold of pearl sugar (also known as nibbed sugar), use flaked/slivered or chopped almonds instead.

300 g/2¼ cups plain/all-purpose flour

1 tablespoon baking powder

a pinch of salt

200 g/¾ cup plus 2 tablespoons cold butter, cut into cubes

125 g/¾ cup plus 2 tablespoons icing/confectioners' sugar

2 teaspoons vanilla sugar

1 egg

1 egg white, lightly beaten, for brushing

pearl sugar or chopped almonds, for sprinkling

MAKES AROUND 40

Mix the flour with the baking powder and a pinch of salt in a bowl. Add the cubed butter and mix with your fingers until it forms crumbs, then add the icing/confectioners' sugar and vanilla sugar and mix again. Add the whole egg and mix until the dough is even (but don't over-mix).

Pop the dough into a bag and leave to settle in the fridge for about an hour.

Preheat the oven to 180°C (350°F) Gas 4. Line several baking sheets with baking parchment.

Cut the dough into around 40 equal pieces (around 15 g/½ oz. each), roll them into small balls, and place on the lined baking sheets. Make sure you leave space around each piece of dough, as they spread out while baking. Using the back of a fork, press each one down gently in the middle to a diameter of around 3 cm/1¼ in. (they will spread more when baking). If you prefer a flat surface, use the bottom of a glass or similar.

Brush the biscuits with the egg white and sprinkle the pearl sugar or chopped almonds over the top.

Bake in the preheated oven for around 10 minutes or until just baked through (don't let them go brown – you want only a slight tinge of colour at the edges). Baking times can vary depending on your oven, so keep an eye on them. Remove from the oven and leave to cool before storing in an airtight container.

sukkerkringler
DANISH BUTTER COOKIES

I haven't counted how many different butter cookies there are in Scandinavia, but there are hundreds and hundreds of different varieties and regional specialities. These particular biscuits are probably better known around the world than many others, as they are often sold in tins decorated with scenes of Copenhagen and labelled 'Danish Butter Cookies'. I quite like these little kringle-shaped ones because the addition of cream to the mixture makes the pastry a little flaky. Note that in Sweden, the similar word *sockerkringlor* can also refer to a more bready variety – there are several versions of these that vary regionally.

250 g/1 cup plus
2 tablespoons butter

375 g/2⅞ cups plain/
all-purpose flour, plus extra
for dusting

150 g/1 cup icing/
confectioners' sugar

1 egg yolk

3–4 tablespoons double/
heavy cream

egg white, lightly beaten,
for brushing

sanding, pearl or demerara/
turbinado sugar, to decorate

MAKES APPROX. 30

Mix the butter and flour together to form crumbs. Add the sugar and mix, then work in the egg yolk and, finally, the cream. If the dough is too sticky, add a little more flour. Don't overwork the dough too much. Leave it to rest in a plastic bag in the fridge for at least an hour until cold.

Preheat the oven to 200°C (400°F) Gas 6. Line two baking sheets with baking parchment.

Turn the dough out onto a floured surface. Roll pieces of around 20–25 g/¾–1 oz. into thin 'sausage' shapes about 20 cm/8 in. long, then form each into a pretzel shape and place on the lined baking sheets (the biscuits will spread out during cooking, so make sure there is space between them). Repeat until all the dough is used.

Brush with egg white and top with the sugar, then bake in the preheated oven for 8–10 minutes until just baked through (don't allow them to brown too much). Leave to cool before storing in an airtight container.

Variations
I use pearl or crystal sugar to decorate these, but you can use finely chopped nuts or demerara/turbinado sugar if you prefer. Sanding or crystal sugar is a bigger cut than demerara – you can buy it in some supermarkets and online. Alternatively, use pearl or nibbed sugar, or, indeed, demerara. I use pearl sugar, but bash it a bit first to break up the biggest lumps. You can also flavour them – a dash of vanilla, cardamom or ginger will spice them up.

snebolde

SNOWBALLS

Across Scandinavia, we spend time preparing a lot of little marzipan treats at Christmas. I love making these because they look pretty and festive on a plate, along with biscuits, cookies and other treats. My kids love making them because they get to spray them with edible silver glitter.

200 g/7 oz. marzipan (63% almond content is the best for these sorts of treats, but you need at least a minimum of 50%)

120 g/4 oz. good-quality white chocolate

100 g/1⅓ cups desiccated/ dried shredded coconut

food-safe silver glitter (optional)

cocktail sticks/toothpicks

MAKES 20

Cut the marzipan into 20 pieces. Roll each piece into a ball, then leave in the fridge so they are cold when you add the chocolate – this allows them to dry quicker.

Temper the white chocolate (see page 61 for instructions – tempering white chocolate can be tricky, but the easiest way is to melt half in a bain-marie, then remove from the heat and stir in the remaining half to cool it down quickly).

Gently insert a cocktail stick/toothpick into a marzipan ball, then dip it in the melted chocolate so that it has a thin covering. Roll the ball in the desiccated/shredded coconut and leave to set on baking parchment. Repeat wth the remaining marzipan balls.

Decorate with a little food-safe silver glitter, if you wish.

Variations
To flavour the marzipan, add a bit of finely grated orange zest when rolling the marzipan. For an adults-only version, 2 tablespoons Amaretto works well. For a more decadent version, roll the marzipan around pieces of Viennese nougat.

vaniljekranse med appelsin
VANILLA & ORANGE BUTTER COOKIES

No Danish Christmas is complete without these ringed butter cookies, famous all over the world. These ones have added orange zest for variation, but if you want to stay traditional, leave it out. These cookies may spread in the oven, and it is quite hard to get them to keep their pattern, so I usually chill them before baking.

170 g/⁷⁄₈ cup granulated sugar

200 g/³⁄₄ cup plus 2 tablespoons butter, at room temperature

275 g/2 cups strong bread flour

100 g/1 cup ground almonds

1 teaspoon baking powder

1 egg

a pinch of salt

seeds from 1 whole vanilla pod/bean

1 teaspoon freshly grated orange zest

a strong piping/pastry bag and a medium star nozzle/tip

MAKES ABOUT 30

Mix the sugar and butter (only briefly until just combined), then add the remaining ingredients and mix until you have an even dough (you can do this in a food processor or by hand). Do not overmix. Your dough needs to be soft enough to push through a piping/pastry bag nozzle. It is a hard dough – in Denmark, most people use a metal case to push the dough through the nozzle. A fabric piping/pastry bag is also good. If you find this difficult but have a good-sized nozzle, you can simply push the dough through the nozzle with your thumb.

Line several baking sheets with baking parchment. Pipe out rolls 8–10 cm/3¼–4 in. long, then carefully connect into circles and place on the lined baking sheets. Make sure the rolls are no thicker than your little finger, because they will spread a bit during baking. Place the baking sheets in the fridge if you have space so they can firm up as much as possible before baking.

Preheat the oven to 200°C (400°F) Gas 6.

Pop a chilled baking sheet of cookies in the preheated oven and bake for 8–10 minutes, or until the slightest tinge of golden brown appears at the edges. Remove from the oven and allow to cool before eating. Repeat until everything is baked. Store in an airtight container.

pebernødder
PEPPERNUTS

While there are no actual nuts (or, generally, pepper) in this recipe for Denmark's unique version of a spiced gingerbread, the cookies are the shape and size of a large hazelnut, which gives them the name. These are essential at Christmas time in Denmark, and in my recipe I've embraced black pepper for a good kick. If you prefer a milder taste, or if these will be eaten by kids, use only white pepper (and go easy on it). I remember making these with my grandmother, followed by a peppernut hunt where I got to eat loads of them. We also used to put these in paper cones on the Christmas tree. These bring back fond memories of snow-filled gardens, warm kitchens and my grandmother's wonderful smile.

200 g/^{3}/$_4$ cup plus
2 tablespoons butter,
at room temperature

200 g/1 cup granulated
sugar

400–425 g/3–3^1/$_4$ cups
plain/all-purpose flour

1 teaspoon baking powder

1 teaspoon bicarbonate of/
baking soda

a pinch of salt

75 ml/5 tablespoons double/
heavy cream

^{1}/$_2$ teaspoon freshly grated
lemon zest (optional)

PEPPERNUT SPICE MIX

^{1}/$_2$ teaspoon ground cloves

1 teaspoon ground ginger

1 teaspoon ground
cardamom

2^1/$_2$ teaspoons ground
cinnamon

1 teaspoon mixed spice/
apple pie spice

^{1}/$_2$ teaspoon white pepper

^{1}/$_2$ teaspoon freshly ground
black pepper (optional)

**MAKES APPROX. 100
SMALL COOKIES**

Cream the butter and sugar together in a mixer, then add the flour, baking powder, bicarbonate of/baking soda, salt and the spice mix. Mix until you have an even dough, then add the cream. Mix again.

Chill the dough in the fridge for at least 30 minutes before using.

Preheat the oven to 200°C (400°F) Gas 6. Line several baking sheets with baking parchment.

Roll out pieces of dough into thumb-sized rolls or cut or shape little pieces about 1.5 cm/^{5}/$_8$ in. in diameter (no bigger) and pop on the lined baking sheets. You will get around 100 from this recipe, so you may want to go with the cut version rather than rolled if you're in a hurry!

Bake in the preheated oven for around 8–10 minutes. Do keep an eye on the baking time, because your oven may vary and these little biscuits need to be only just golden, not any darker.

Leave to cool before eating so that they can crisp up. Store in an airtight container.

havregrynskugler / chokladbollar
CHOCOLATE & OAT BALLS

All Scandinavian kids know this basic chocolate treat recipe. It requires no baking
and is super-quick to make, as it's essentially butter, cocoa and sugar! In Sweden and
Norway, these are made all year round, but they're usually kept for the festive season
in Denmark. Make these ahead and keep them in the fridge, as they last for a week or so.
I tend to make a few batches and flavour them for different tastes, either flavouring the
balls as I make them or rolling them in flavoured coverings. Colourful sprinkles and
gentle flavours suit kids, but for a grown-up version, alcohol and more coffee work well.
Make a large quantity, split the mixture into several batches (I normally do four batches
of around 200 g/7 oz. each) and flavour each one at the end. I've included some favourite
variations below, but this recipe is perfect for experimentation.

**250 g/1 cup plus
2 tablespoons butter,
softened**

**400 g/4 cups rolled/
old-fashioned oats**

**150 g/1 cup icing/
confectioners' sugar**

**3–4 heaped tablespoons
cocoa powder**

**4 tablespoons brewed
strong coffee, cooled**

1 teaspoon vanilla sugar

MAKES AROUND 30–40

Place all the ingredients in a mixing bowl and mix until you have a
good, uniform mixture. I usually do it in a stand mixer with a paddle
attachment, but this isn't difficult to do by hand.

Make equal-sized balls (usually the size of a whole walnut), then roll
in your chosen covering (see below), before chilling in the fridge. The
traditional treat is simply rolled in pearl/nibbed sugar, desiccated/dried
shredded coconut or hundreds and thousands/sprinkles.

Flavours and coverings

Orange: This one is for the grown-ups only. Add 2 tablespoons
Cointreau and $\frac{1}{4}$ teaspoon finely grated orange zest to 200 g/7 oz.
of your mixture. Roll in chocolate sprinkles.

Almond: Another adults-only one. Add 2 tablespoons Amaretto to
200 g/7 oz. of your mixture, then roll in toasted, chopped almonds.

Raspberry: Children can enjoy this one. Add 1 tablespoon raspberry
jam/preserves to 200 g/7 oz. of your mixture. Roll in freeze-dried
raspberry pieces or chocolate sprinkles.

klejner
FRIED PASTRIES

One of my favourite Christmas treats has always been freshly baked *klejner*, a really old treat dating back to the Middle Ages. As with all recipes, this has developed across the lands. In Iceland, it is slightly different from Denmark, and different also from the Norwegian version. In Sweden, it is mostly popular in the south, and rarely eaten up north. Food travels and changes. This is the Norwegian version, but if you would prefer to try the Danish version, you will find it on my food blog.

200 ml/³/₄ cup lukewarm whole milk

25 g/⁷/₈ oz. fresh yeast

75 g/6 tablespoons caster/superfine sugar

50 g/3¹/₂ tablespoons butter, softened

1 egg

300 g/2 cups plus 2 tablespoons strong bread flour, plus extra for dusting

¹/₂ teaspoon salt

1 teaspoon ground cardamom

freshly grated zest of 1 lemon

500 ml/2 cups coconut oil (or any oil with a high smoking point), for frying

icing/confectioners' sugar, for dusting

MAKES APPROX. 20

In a stand mixer, combine the lukewarm milk and yeast until dissolved, then add the sugar and stir again. Add the soft butter and egg, then start adding the flour, salt and cardamom, followed by the zest. You may not need all the flour, or you may need a bit more. Knead for around 3–4 minutes – it shouldn't be runny or too sticky, but slightly springy. Leave in a covered bowl to rise for about an hour.

When you're ready to cook the *klejner*, heat the coconut oil in a deep pan to 180°C/350°F.

Roll out the dough on a floured surface, to a thickness of around 5 mm/¹/₄ in. Using a pastry wheel, cut into strips around 5 cm/2 in. wide, then cut at an angle, but a bit longer (6 cm/2¹/₂ in.) so you end up with diamond shapes. Cut a slit in the middle of each one. To make the knot, pull one corner of the pastry through the hole in the middle and pull gently.

Carefully drop the *klejner* into the hot oil and fry, turning over halfway. Each will take 1¹/₂–2 minutes. You will need to cook them in batches. Drain on paper towels and dust lightly with icing/confectioners' sugar. These are best eaten on the day you make them.

pepparkakor
SWEDISH GINGER BISCUITS

These are probably the most famous treat to come out of Sweden (besides the Plopp chocolate bar). This recipe is a quick dough which is easy to roll out so the kids can make lots of festive shapes. Every December, families across Scandinavia will sit around a table with a batch of dough, festive music on, making loads of cookies and baked goods for all the coming Sundays of Advent.

550 g/4¼ cups plain/all-purpose flour, plus extra for dusting

1 teaspoon bicarbonate of/baking soda

1½ teaspoons ground ginger

1 teaspoon ground cloves

1 tablespoon ground cinnamon

1 teaspoon ground cardamom

½ teaspoon ground allspice

a pinch of salt

100 g/½ cup granulated sugar

100 g/½ cup soft dark brown sugar

150 g/⅔ cup butter, at room temperature

200 g/⅔ cup golden/corn syrup

150 ml/⅔ cup double/heavy cream

MAKES 50–70

In a stand mixer fitted with the paddle attachment, mix the flour, bicarbonate of/baking soda, spices, salt and sugars together. Add the rest of the ingredients, and mix until you have an even dough. Shape it into a log and wrap in clingfilm/plastic wrap. Rest it in the fridge at least overnight before using – try to resist eating the dough while it's chilling!

Preheat the oven to 200°C (400°F) Gas 6. Line several baking sheets with baking parchment.

On a floured surface, roll out the dough very thinly (around 2 mm/⅛ in. thick), and use cookie cutters to cut your desired shapes. Make sure they are thin biscuits. Place them on the lined baking sheets.

Bake in the preheated oven – each batch will take 5–6 minutes, depending on the thickness. The biscuits should be a darker shade of brown without being burnt. Remove from the oven and leave to cool before storing in an airtight container.

If you wish, you can let the kids loose with colourful icing/frosting. Icing/confectioners' sugar mixed with beaten egg white and a few drops of freshly squeezed lemon juice makes the best decorative icing as it goes hard when it dries.

brunkager
MORMOR'S DANISH BISCUITS

Sweden might be famous for its *pepparkaka* spiced biscuit, but in Denmark, every household bakes *brunkager* ('brown biscuits') instead. These are quite closely related to their Swedish cousin, but are a little more spicy and have added nuts (and, sometimes, candied peel – which you can omit if you are not keen on it).

My *mormor* (or grandmother) Erna used to bake a massive amount of these every Christmas in the traditional way – rolling the dough into logs, chilling them, then simply slicing and placing onto baking sheets. The work is quickly done if you need to make enough to last throughout the whole festive season. This is a hard dough, not suitable for rolling flat and using cutters.

150 g/scant ¹/₂ cup golden/corn syrup

250 g/1 cup plus 2 tablespoons butter

150 g/³/₄ cup granulated sugar

75 g/¹/₃ cup dark muscovado sugar

500 g/3³/₄ cups plain/all-purpose flour

2 teaspoons ground cinnamon

1¹/₂ teaspoons ground ginger

1 teaspoon ground cloves

1 teaspoon ground cardamom

1¹/₂ teaspoons bicarbonate of/baking soda

a pinch of salt

100 g/³/₄ cup chopped almonds

75 g/¹/₂ cup candied peel, chopped (optional)

MAKES 100+ BISCUITS

In a saucepan, melt the golden/corn syrup, butter and both sugars until melted, taking care not to overheat. Leave to cool for about 10 minutes.

Mix 400 g/3 cups of the flour with the spices, bicarbonate of/baking soda and salt. Add the chopped nuts (and candied peel, if using), then add the melted sugar mixture. Add more flour as needed – you need to mix well to have a smooth, even dough.

Shape into logs around 4 cm/1¹/₂ in. in diameter, then wrap in clingfilm/plastic wrap and chill completely in the fridge. Ideally, do this overnight (or for longer, to allow the flavours to really develop). You can also freeze the dough after chilling and carefully slice from frozen if you have a super-sharp knife.

To bake, preheat the oven to 175°C (350°F) Gas 4. Line several baking sheets with baking parchment.

Slice the biscuits thinly – about 1.5–2 mm/¹/₈ in. – and place on the lined baking sheets, leaving a little space between them. Bake in the preheated oven for 5–8 minutes, or until browned all over (but not dark brown around the edges). Leave to cool and crisp up before transferring to an airtight container.

daimtryffel
EASY DAIM TRUFFLES

Who doesn't love Daim bars? Loved the world over, these almond crunch bars are synonymous with Swedish confectionery. I love using them in my Christmas treats.

200 ml/³/₄ cup double/
heavy cream

180 g/6¹/₂ oz. dark/
bittersweet chocolate,
chopped

50 g/3¹/₂ tablespoons butter

1–2 tablespoons cognac, or
similar (optional, for adult
truffles)

2 Daim bars (28 g/1 oz.
each), finely chopped

good-quality cocoa powder,
to dust and roll

MAKES APPROX. 30

In a saucepan, heat the cream to boiling point, then turn off the heat and add the chocolate. Once it has melted, add the butter and cognac, if using, and allow to melt and combine.

Transfer to a bowl and leave to cool to room temperature, then add the chopped Daim bars and stir. Allow to cool further before shaping into balls of around 20 g/³/₄ oz. each. This is slightly messy, but I do find doing it by hand works well, while others prefer to use a melon baller. Once rolled to a uniform shape, roll in cocoa powder. Leave to set and harden up for several hours.

If you keep them chilled, you will need to bring the truffles to room temperature before serving. Mine don't usually last that long!

pepparkaka cookies

GOOEY GINGERBREAD COOKIES

There's something comforting about a gooey cookie. These are not native to the Nordic region, but we make these in the café at Christmas time because they taste like Scandi ginger biscuits. They're moreish and perfect with a cup of hot glögg or hot chocolate. They probably taste a bit like gingerbread dough, which is something we secretly love to eat.

150 g/²/₃ cup butter

300 g/2¼ cups plain/all-purpose flour

1 teaspoon bicarbonate of/baking soda

½ teaspoon sea salt flakes

150 g/³/₄ cup soft brown sugar

100 g/½ cup caster/superfine sugar

1 egg and 1 egg yolk

3 tablespoons milk

NORDIC GINGER BISCUIT SPICE MIX

2 teaspoons ground cinnamon

1 teaspoon ground ginger

½ teaspoon ground cloves

½ teaspoon ground cardamom

½ teaspoon vanilla sugar

50 g/2 oz. roughly chopped macadamia nuts

MAKES 15 (DEPENDING ON HOW MUCH DOUGH YOU EAT)

Melt the butter and set aside to cool.

Combine the flour, bicarbonate of/baking soda, salt and spice mix in a bowl, then set aside.

Combine the brown and caster/superfine sugars with the cooled, melted butter, and stir until no lumps remain. Combine the egg, egg yolk and milk, then mix with the sugars and butter until thoroughly combined. Add the flour mixture little by little until everything is incorporated, then chill the dough in the fridge for a few hours.

Preheat the oven to 175°C (350°F) Gas 4. Line several baking sheets with baking parchment.

Form the dough into rough balls about the size of a golf ball. Place the balls about 5 cm/2 in. apart on the lined baking sheets (they will spread during baking).

Bake in the preheated oven for 8½–10 minutes or until just golden, then remove from the oven immediately and transfer to a wire rack. The middle should still be slightly soft when you take them out of the oven, and they will harden up after a while. The cookies will be best after cooling for about 30 minutes – slightly warm, but chewy in the middle.

joulutorttu
FINNISH JAM STARS

Riina in the café loves these easy treats from her homeland at Christmas. The traditional recipe for the pastry is quite fiddly and includes ricotta, cream and butter, but as everybody is so busy at Christmas, a lot of people just make these with their children using ready-made puff pastry. They take just 5–10 minutes to whip up and cut the shapes. Traditionally, a prune filling is used, but we have made these with all kinds of compote (including lingonberry and blueberry). If you want to use jam/preserves with a high sugar content, add a little cornflour/cornstarch to avoid the sugar melting and spilling out in your oven.

1 sheet of shop-bought puff pastry (the sheet I used measured approx. 30 x 18 cm/ 12 x 7 in., which produced 15 squares of 6 x 6 cm/ 2^1/$_2$ x 2^1/$_2$ in.)

beaten egg, for brushing

icing/confectioners' sugar, for dusting

PRUNE FILLING
150 g/5^1/$_2$ oz. dried pitted prunes

50 g/^{1}/$_4$ cup sugar (or more, to taste)

1–2 tablespoons freshly squeezed lemon juice

MAKES 15

To make the filling, place the prunes, sugar and lemon juice in a small saucepan with water just covering them, and bring to a slow simmer. Cook for around 20 minutes or until the prunes are really soft. Purée if needed, then cool and use as directed.

Preheat the oven to 175°C (350°F) Gas 4. Line two baking sheets with baking parchment.

Cut the pastry into 15 equal squares of around 6 x 6 cm/2^1/$_2$ x 2^1/$_2$ in. (the size is not important – if your sheet is a different size, just cut into equal squares close to this size). On each square, make a diagonal cut from each corner towards the middle, stopping 1 cm/^{1}/$_2$ in. from the centre.

Brush each square with beaten egg, then transfer each one to the lined baking sheets. Add 1 teaspoon of the prune filling (or jam/ preserves, if you prefer) in the centre, then fold one corner into the middle, repeating all the way around to form a little star. In total, you'll probably need around 150 g/5^1/$_2$ oz. of filling or jam.

Bake in the preheated oven for 12–15 minutes until the pastry has cooked through and is golden and puffed up. Allow to cool down a little before dusting with icing/confectioners' sugar and serving.

konfekt
MARZIPAN TREATS

A lot of marzipan and nougat is consumed in Scandinavia over Christmas. In Denmark, the word *konfekt* covers any bite-sized treats, from marzipan to truffles and toffees. My mother used to make lots of different kinds of *konfekt* with us in the week before Christmas.

250 g/9 oz. marzipan (a minimum of 60% almonds)

icing/confectioners' sugar, for rolling

100 g/3¹/₂ oz. Viennese nougat

100–150 g/3¹/₂–5¹/₂ oz. dark/bittersweet chocolate, tempered (see page 61)

edible gold leaf or freeze-dried raspberries, to decorate

MAKES 20–25

Roll out the marzipan to 5-mm/¹/₄-in. thickness – dust the work surface with icing/confectioners' sugar to stop it sticking. Roll out the nougat to 5-mm/¹/₄-in. thickness and place over half of the marzipan (if it's too sticky, put it in the fridge to firm up). Cover the top of the nougat with the other half of the marzipan. Roll gently with the rolling pin to combine the layers ever so slightly – again, use icing/confectioners' sugar if it's sticky. Trim the edges to get a neat shape.

Cut into diamonds (or as desired) and cover lightly with tempered chocolate, then leave to harden. Decorate with a little edible gold leaf or freeze-dried raspberries. As a variation, try adding cognac-soaked raisins or other flavourings to your marzipan.

p-toerter
PEANUT TARTS

I loved these treats when I was a child – French nougat with salted peanuts and chocolate. Years later, I wondered why we call them 'P-tarts' in Denmark. It turns out that it's just because they look like little tartlets, and the 'P' stands for peanuts in English. I've included my method for French nougat, but you can simply buy French nougat pieces if you wish.

200–250 g/1¹/₄–2 cups salted peanuts

100 g/3¹/₂ oz. good-quality chocolate – I like to use ²/₃ dark/bittersweet and ¹/₃ milk chocolate (but just use dark/ bittersweet if you prefer)

Get everything ready as you're working against the clock. Line your baking pan for setting the nougat with baking parchment and a little non-stick spray (or rice paper is ideal, and more traditional).

For the nougat, place the sugar and glucose in a pan with 50 ml/3¹/₂ tablespoons water. Heat carefully until the sugar has melted, then turn up the heat to 130°C/266°F (soft ball stage on a sugar

FRENCH NOUGAT

400 g/2 cups caster/
superfine sugar, plus
$^1/_2$ teaspoon

75 g/5 tablespoons liquid
glucose

300 g/1$^1/_4$ cups clear, runny
honey

2 egg whites (approx.
60-65 g/2$^1/_4$ oz.)

*20 x 30-cm/8 x 12-in.
baking pan, ideally with
sides 1.5 cm/$^5/_8$ in. tall*

sugar/candy thermometer

**MAKES AROUND
40-50 PIECES (THE
RECIPE CAN BE HALVED)**

thermometer). Also bring the honey to the boil in a separate pan (this won't take long). Now turn up the heat on the sugar and increase the temperature to exactly 158°C/316°F (hard crack stage). Move the pan off the heat (this will allow the sugar to reduce to around 145°C/293°F).

As you are doing this, in a completely clean bowl whisk the egg whites with $^1/_2$ teaspoon caster/superfine sugar until they form stiff peaks.

Once the egg white is stiff, steadily add the hot honey while whisking on medium speed. The honey will cook the egg whites (your bowl will become hot – this is essential). When this is incorporated, start to add the sugar syrup (which has reduced to around 145°C/293°F after being taken off the heat) in a slow but steady stream, on medium speed (taking care NOT to hit the bowl or beaters – aim for inbetween). This may take a little while – don't add too quickly, be steady about it.

Once added, turn the mixer speed to high and beat for 5–7 minutes until the mixture is very glossy, smooth and fairly thick. This beating time is essential – if you do not beat for long enough, your finished mix will be runny. Your mixer may sound like it's about to give up: this is hard work. I use a whisk, but some people find a paddle attachment is easier. Once done, add half the nuts and beat only to incorporate.

Roll or press the mixture into the prepared baking pan, to a thickness of about 1.5 cm/$^5/_8$ in. Press all remaining peanuts on top all across the surface. Cover with a piece of baking parchment (with cake release spray on) and use a rolling pin to flatten the surface completely and press out any air. Leave to cool for at least 3 hours, or ideally overnight.

Temper the chocolate (this means to heat the chocolate to a certain degree so that when set it forms a pleasing crack when you bite into it). There are several ways to do this, but this is my quick home method. Melt half the chocolate in a very clean, dry, heatproof bowl set over a bain-marie until the chocolate is just liquid, then dab a little on the inside of your wrist (a heat-sensitive area) – it should feel warm but not burning hot. Take the bowl off the bain-marie and quickly stir in the remaining chocolate. This will melt and bring down the temperature of the whole bowl and help to temper it.

Spread or pipe the chocolate over the surface of the nougat and leave for 15–20 minutes to set, then cut into bite-sized pieces. It can be tricky to cut – it's easiest to use an oiled, sharp knife.

If your nougat has set too soft (this can happen in a humid room, if you have not beaten it enough or if the sugar did not reach 158°C/316°F), cut the pieces out, then dip into melted chocolate and leave to set. It will still taste delicious, so don't fret – it happens to the best of us.

knäck

SWEDISH TOFFEE

Every household in Sweden makes *knäck* at Christmas – little soft toffees. In my house, we flavour them lots of different ways, and use little petit-four cases. Just remember to use cases that are lined, or else they will stick. You can also give them a quick spray of cake-release spray before filling with the toffee, just to make sure.

200 g/²/₃ cup golden/corn syrup

160 g/³/₄ cup plus
1 tablespoon caster/
superfine sugar

200 ml/³/₄ cup whipping cream

50 g/3¹/₂ tablespoons butter

sugar/candy thermometer

petit-four cases

**MAKES APPROX.
30 LITTLE TOFFEES,
DEPENDING ON THE
SIZE OF THE CASES**

You will need to use a large saucepan as the mixture will bubble up a lot during cooking.

Place the syrup, sugar and whipping cream in a large saucepan and bring to the boil over a medium heat. You need to keep an eye on it all the time – I can't emphasize this enough. The temperature needs to reach exactly 125°C/257°F. Along the way to that point, it will bubble – then, right before it hits 125°C/257°F, it will start to turn brown. This whole process can take 20–25 minutes, so make sure you won't be distracted.

As soon as you have the exact temperature, take the pan off the heat and stir in the butter. If you leave it to cook for any longer, the finished toffee will be too hard. If you take it off the heat before 125°C/257°F, you end up with a fudge-style finish.

Leave it for a few minutes. At this stage, you can split it into several different bowls in order to add different flavourings, or you can simply portion it out and add flavours to the top of the warm toffee before it goes hard. I have not included quantities for the fillings here as tastes are different, but for a full recipe consider around 75 g/3 oz. of nuts or seeds; for spices, a few teaspoons should suffice.

When the mixture has cooled a little, pour into plastic piping/pastry bags or a pourer, and pipe into the little petit-four cases. Add the flavourings to the top, then leave to cool down and harden up.

Flavour suggestions
Sesame seeds and flaked sea salt
2 teaspoons cocoa powder
Chopped toasted almonds
Chopped pistachios
Pine nuts
Liquorice powder
Vanilla (add vanilla sugar and a pinch of sea salt
to the hot toffee before portioning)

CHRISTMAS EVE

The biggest day of the Scandinavian Yuletide – and probably the entire year. As the sun sets, streets go quiet and dinner is prepared to the exact same specifications as every Christmas Eve before. We feast and then light the candles on the tree, wishing each other *god jul!*

ROLLED TURKEY WITH MEATBALL STUFFING

Having lived abroad for so long, Christmas for me is all about traditional food from home. Of course, living in the UK, British traditions have influenced our family, so we are partial to turkey at Christmas – with a Scandi twist, of course. Roasting a whole turkey is hard to do well, so I prefer to use sections of the bird to control the cooking better. Here I have mixed it up and settled on a marriage of Swedish and British flavours.

1.5–2 kg/3¼–4½ lb. boneless turkey breast with the skin on – ask the butcher to cut a one-piece turkey breast and then butterfly it for you (the ones in the supermarket are usually made from several smaller pieces)

3 tablespoons freshly chopped parsley

3 tablespoons freshly chopped thyme

approx. ½ of the Swedish meatball mixture, uncooked (see page 103)

100–120 g/3½–4 oz. thinly sliced pancetta (you can use streaky bacon, but the thicker the slices, the more you'll need, as it needs to cover the whole roast)

a knob of butter

a glug of oil, for frying

salt and freshly ground black pepper

butcher's string

meat thermometer

SERVES 6

Carefully remove the skin from the turkey breast and set to one side. If your butcher hasn't already done so, use a sharp knife to butterfly the turkey breast – turn the breast over so the side that had the skin is down, then slice into the thickest part of the breast with the knife parallel to your chopping board so that you can 'open' the breast up, like a book. Remove any cartilage or other unwanted bits, and cut into any really thick sections to open further. Cover the top with clingfilm/plastic wrap and beat with a mallet or rolling pin so you end up with a thickness of around 1 cm/½ in. all over, and ideally a piece of meat that measures approx. 20 x 25 cm/8 x 10 in.

Cover the meat with the herbs and season. Spread the meatball mixture evenly over the meat to a thickness of 1 cm/½ in. You may have some left over, but don't be tempted to use it up. Carefully roll the turkey tightly, placing the turkey skin lengthways over the opening to help keep it closed. Cover the turkey all over with pancetta slices. Using the butcher's string, tie up the turkey firmly and evenly all along at intervals of 1.5 cm/⅝ in., and twice lengthways.

Preheat the oven to 175°C (350°F) Gas 4.

Melt a knob of butter with a glug of oil in a frying pan/skillet, then quickly brown the turkey on all sides. Transfer to a roasting pan, place in the middle of the oven and roast until done. This will take anything from 50 to 70 minutes, depending on the bird, the thickness of the meat and your oven. A good guide is around 15 minutes per 500 g/1 lb. 2 oz., plus an extra 15 minutes (for a 1.5-kg/3¼-lb. roll, that's around 60 minutes). The turkey is cooked once the internal temperature reaches 72°C (162°F) on a meat thermometer.

Remove from the oven, rest for at least 15 minutes, then remove the string and carve. Resting should bring the internal temperature to 74–75°C (165–167°F) – any higher and the meat will start to feel dry. Serve with gravy made from roasting-pan juices, Hasselback Potatoes (see page 81), Raw Stirred Lingonberries (see page 85) and vegetables.

hjorteskank / hjortlägg
VENISON SHANK

Venison is much easier to buy than reindeer outside the Nordic countries, so I often use this as a substitute – in many recipes you can simply replace one for the other. However, if you do find reindeer, do try it. Both venison and reindeer shanks almost cook themselves – there's no need to do much other than set aside the time to cook them.

4 medium shanks
of venison or reindeer

a large knob of butter

a glug of olive oil

3 slices of streaky bacon,
or similar, chopped

10–12 juniper berries,
crushed

2 carrots, cut into chunks

2 small onions, roughly
chopped

1 parsnip, cut into chunks

1 celery stick/stalk, roughly
chopped

100 g/3$^{1}/_{2}$ oz. (approx.)
celeriac, peeled and roughly
chopped

plain/all-purpose flour

300 ml/1$^{1}/_{4}$ cups red wine

1 bay leaf

4–5 sprigs of fresh thyme

600–700 ml/2$^{1}/_{2}$–3 cups
beef or game stock

salt and freshly ground
black pepper

SERVES 4

Preheat the oven to 160°C (325°F) Gas 3.

Season the shanks all over with salt and pepper. Heat a large ovenproof casserole dish on the hob/stovetop, and melt the butter with a glug of olive oil. Add the shanks, brown them all over and set aside. Fry the bacon and crushed juniper berries in the same fat and leave them in the dish.

Add the vegetables to the dish and cook until they start to go soft. Return the meat to the dish, then scatter over a tablespoon of flour. Add the red wine and cook for a few minutes. Add more seasoning, along with the bay leaf, thyme and stock, then cover with the lid. Pop the dish in the oven for 4 hours, checking it every once in a while. You just need to let it cook slowly.

After the cooking time is up, carefully remove the shanks from the dish and cover with foil. Strain the cooking sauce to remove the vegetables and thicken it with flour to make a sauce. Season the sauce as needed.

Serve one shank per person with mashed potato (good with a dollop of grainy mustard stirred in) and Raw Stirred Lingonberries (see page 85) on the side. If you want an additional side dish, I recommend Jutlandic Stewed Kale (see page 96) or Red Cabbage (see page 74).

flæskesteg / ribbe
ROAST PORK

Traditionally, a lot of people in Denmark and parts of Norway eat roast pork for their Christmas Eve dinner. The cuts of meat used are different, but the roasting method is the same, so I've included Danish *flæskesteg* and Norwegian *ribbe* here as one recipe.

2-kg/4^1/$_2$-lb. piece of pork*
salt
bay leaves
whole cloves

meat thermometer

SERVES 6-7

* *Flæskesteg* is most often made using sirloin of pork, which has less fat than the belly cut of *ribbe*. Both are roasted in the oven until done, then the crackling is given a serious amount of heat to puff it up before carving. We never separate the crackling from the meat while cooking - it's left on.

For *ribbe*, buy a 2-kg/4^1/$_2$-lb. meaty pork belly piece with the bones underneath. Ask your butcher to score it in 1-cm/^{1}/$_2$-in. crosses through the fat, but not touching the meat. For *flæskesteg*, buy a 2-kg/4^1/$_2$-lb. pork sirloin, not rolled, but flat with the bones removed. Ask the butcher to score the rind at 1-cm/^{1}/$_2$-in. slices all the way across, through the fat, but not quite touching the meat. Alternatively, you can score it yourself with a small knife and a bit of determination.

Preheat the oven to 200°C (400°F) Gas 6.

Add hot water to a roasting pan and place your pork, skin-side down, in the water. The water should be approx. 1-1.5 cm/^{1}/$_2$-^{5}/$_8$ in. deep and just about cover the fatty rind.

Place in the hot oven for about 20 minutes, then remove. Discard the water and turn the pork over - this will separate the fatty top bits and allow for easier crackling later on.

Pat the rind dry with paper towels, then salt liberally all over, ensuring the cracks are salted too. Insert a few bay leaves and cloves in the rind cracks. Add about 475 ml/2 scant cups of water to the roasting pan, then return to the oven, reducing the temperature to 130°C (275°F) Gas 1. The pork will now need to roast for anything between 1^1/$_2$ and 2 hours before reaching an internal temperature of 68°C (154°F).

Once the meat is at the correct temperature, preheat the grill/broiler and place the pork underneath. Keep an eye on it - crackling burns easily so you may need to move it around under the heat until you have a crispy crackling. Use a meat thermometer to check that the temperature has risen above 72°C (162°F) in the thickest part of the meat at this stage.

Leave to rest for at least 15 minutes before carving. Reserve the juices in the roasting pan for the gravy (see page 85).

For *flæskesteg*, slices the size of one crackling rind are served; for *ribbe*, rectangular pieces are cut at a size of around 6 x 5 cm/2^1/$_2$ x 2 in. It can be difficult to cut through the bones in *ribbe* so ask your butcher to do this for you beforehand.

Serve *flæskesteg* with boiled and Browned Potatoes (see page 81), Thick Pork Gravy (see page 85) and Red Cabbage (see page 74). Serve *ribbe* with boiled potatoes, Thick Pork Gravy, Red Cabbage, Sour Cabbage (see page 74), Norwegian Meatballs (see page 102) and Norwegian sausages.

The pork also makes a great topping for open sandwiches, and is a brilliant ingredient for a potato and meat hash made from leftovers.

kålrabistappe
NORWEGIAN MASHED SWEDE

Swede/rutabaga is an immensely popular root vegetable in Scandinavia. At Christmas Norwegians serve it mashed with traditional dried and salted lamb ribs, but it also works very well for other dishes. In Sweden, a variation of this dish is called *rotmos*, adding a few potatoes to the swede to bring a more starchy result.

1 swede/rutabaga, weighing around 1 kg/2$\frac{1}{4}$ lb.

2 carrots

50 g/3$\frac{1}{2}$ tablespoons butter

100 ml/$\frac{1}{3}$ cup double/heavy cream

freshly grated nutmeg

100 ml/$\frac{1}{3}$ cup meat stock (optional – the stock from the roast pork on page 70 is especially good for this)

salt and freshly ground black pepper

fresh thyme, to garnish

SERVES 4

Peel and cut the swede/rutabaga and carrots into equal-sized pieces, place in a pan and cover with water. Bring to the boil and cook until they're soft.

Remove the vegetables from the pan, making sure you reserve the cooking water. Keep the vegetables warm by covering them with foil if you can't mash them immediately.

Using a masher, add the butter, cream and nutmeg to the vegetables and mash until smooth. Taste, and add the cooking water (and the stock, if using) to taste. If you prefer a smoother mash, you can blitz it in a food processor or with a stick blender. Season to taste, sprinkle with thyme leaves and serve.

lanttulaatikko
FINNISH MASHED SWEDE

This dish from Finland is a gorgeous variation of the Norwegian swede/rutabaga recipe on the left. It goes so beautifully with salty ham or other wintery meals.

1 quantity of the Norwegian Mashed Swede (see left)

1 egg

2 tablespoons maple syrup or dark syrup

$\frac{1}{2}$ teaspoon ground ginger

50 g/$\frac{5}{8}$ cup dried breadcrumbs

SERVES 4

Preheat the oven to 160°C (325°F) Gas 3.

Mix the mashed swede/rutabaga with all the other ingredients, holding back half of the breadcrumbs. Place in an ovenproof dish, then add the remaining breadcrumbs on top.

Bake in the preheated oven for 30–40 minutes until hot and the top has gone a bit crispy.

rødkål
RED CABBAGE

The smell of red cabbage cooking instantly makes me feel at home and, if I close my eyes, I can almost be back in my childhood Christmas Eves. Red cabbage is a staple in all Nordic countries at Christmas and the days that follow. During the rest of the year, we use it as a side for meatballs or on open sandwiches. Red cabbage needs to be cooked longer than most other varieties, so I usually make this the day before, to save time and to allow the flavours to develop.

1 small red cabbage (approx. 800 g/ 1 lb. 12 oz.), chopped

1 apple, peeled, cored and grated

50 g/3½ tablespoons butter

50 g/¼ cup sugar

100 ml/⅓ cup undiluted blackcurrant cordial and 100 ml/⅓ cup water (redcurrant jelly can also be used)

50 ml/3½ tablespoons red or white wine vinegar

salt and freshly ground black pepper

spices, to taste – star anise, bay leaf and allspice are all good options. My usual preference is a cinnamon stick and a very small bit of clove (discard any hard spices before serving)

SERVES 4–6

Place all the ingredients in a saucepan and bring to the boil. Turn down the heat and simmer, covered, for about 2½ hours. Check it from time to time to see if it needs topping up with water.

Once the cooking time is up, check the seasoning, then leave to simmer, uncovered, for a further 30 minutes (again, check the water levels regularly). Season once more and check if the red cabbage needs more salt, vinegar or sugar to taste. You need a good balance of not too sour and not too sweet.

surkål
SOUR CABBAGE

On every Norwegian Christmas table you'll find *surkål* – a homely side dish of sour cabbage Norwegians associate with winter. *Surkål* is often compared to sauerkraut, but it isn't fermented and doesn't take as long to make. Although the old *surkål* recipes are indeed similar to sauerkraut, this quick version is usually standard today. It's easy to achieve a balance between sweet and sour by adjusting the seasoning during cooking. If you're not keen on caraway seeds, use your preferred spices (cumin seeds are good). Make a day ahead for the best flavour – it keeps for about a week in the fridge.

1 small white cabbage (around 800 g/ 1 lb. 12 oz.), chopped

1 tart apple, peeled, cored and grated

40 g/3¼ tablespoons granulated sugar

50 ml/3½ tablespoons white wine vinegar

1 teaspoon caraway seeds (or more to taste)

salt, to taste

SERVES 4–6

Place the cabbage and apple in a saucepan with 250 ml/1 cup water and bring to the boil. Add the sugar and vinegar, the seeds and some salt. Cook, uncovered, over a medium heat for about 30 minutes. Make sure the pan does not boil dry. Check the softness of the cabbage and the seasoning – adjust if necessary to find your own balance between sweet and sour. Add more sugar or vinegar to taste as you wish. If you have any strong meat stock, you can also add this (the pork stock from page 70 is excellent).

Cook for a further 20 minutes or so, uncovered. It may be necessary to top up with a little water along the way if it evaporates too much.

Christmas Eve Traditions

In Scandinavia, the biggest day of the season is Christmas Eve. This is the day when all the most important things happen, including presents and the main meal.

For the pagans, the winter solstice was marked with three days of celebrations when the sun was at its lowest. I once read somewhere that the Vikings celebrated a new day starting when the previous one ended at sundown, which fits nicely with celebrating on Christmas Eve rather than Christmas Day. Whatever the truth, I do know that heading out to a bar or pub for a drink with friends is unheard of in Scandinavia. This is an evening to be spent at home with the people you love the most.

Christmas Eve in most Scandinavian households begins with a filling breakfast to keep you going all day. For the religious, church follows in the late morning. It can be a packed affair, so services tend to be shorter to fit everyone in.

In the early afternoon, food starts to be prepared – the meats usually need several hours to be ready for the dinner.

While we share many traditions in Scandinavia, it is a huge area so food varies greatly from region to region, especially when it comes to Christmas dinner. In some parts of Norway, a steamed rack of lamb called *pinnekjøtt* is served, while others enjoy a roast belly of pork. *Lutefisk*, a gelatinous salted fish, is also eaten (although I'm unsure if it's enjoyed). In Denmark, most people have roast duck or roast sirloin of pork with caramelized potatoes and red cabbage. In Sweden, a large Christmas *smörgåsbord* features a ham or ribs as the centrepiece. Dinner starts in the late afternoon or early evening, and it's a slow affair.

Despite such a big meal, dessert is still rich and creamy – a cold, creamed rice pudding with one whole almond hidden inside. If you find it, you'll be given a prize, usually a marzipan pig or a box of chocolates. My father nearly always wins and nobody is ever quite sure how he does it, although since the addition of grandchildren, he seems to be winning less (but smiling more)! The children all know that presents will arrive after dessert has been eaten.

A bowl of hot rice pudding will also be placed in the attic or basement, to keep the Christmas Elf happy. Across Scandinavia, little elves take care of our homes (and farms) throughout the year. and if you forget to treat them well at Christmas, you run the risk of your house elf playing tricks on you in the year ahead. Ever wondered why you have so many single socks? You will find elves all over our homes during Christmas in the form of little pictures, figurines and decorations.

In some places, the Christmas Elf might actually turn up in person to share out gifts. While the elf's costume usually bears a remarkable similarity to Father Christmas' outfit (the male *nisse* or *tomte* wears red and grey clothes), he is still the Christmas Elf. He also looks suspiciously like grandad or an uncle, but when gifts are handed out, such questions are soon forgotten. In Denmark, the wait for gifts is slightly longer as the Christmas tree is moved to the middle of the room and the real candles on it are lit. Everyone holds hands and dances around the tree singing Christmas songs, then we settle down for the chaos of present-giving and hugs.

While the kids play with their presents until they collapse on the floor in exhaustion, the adults sit around and force-feed each other Christmas biscuits, glögg and other tipples. My whole year builds up to that moment – and I exhale and realize that everything is just as it should be.

juleand
DANISH CHRISTMAS ROAST DUCK

We've always had both duck and roast pork on Christmas Eve – as a big family with different tastes, a bit of both suits us fine. To avoid ending up with a dry bird, buy a plump duck and roast it slowly for a long time at a low temperature. It can be cooked the day before, cut into pieces, then stored in the fridge until you are ready to reheat it. The stuffing is only used to keep the duck moist when cooking.

1 duck, about 3 kg/6³/₄ lb.

3 apples (sour is best, such as Granny Smith)

2 handfuls of dried pitted prunes (approx. 200 g/7 oz.)

¹/₂ orange

salt and freshly ground black pepper

butcher's string or meat pins

roasting pan with a rack

meat thermometer

SERVES 4

Make sure the duck is clean of any straggly bits, inside and out. Reserve the giblets and cut the end wing tips off (there's no meat there, but save them for the gravy – see page 84). Pat the bird dry using paper towels.

Peel and chop the apples and stuff the duck's cavity full to the brim with them, as well as the prunes and the orange half. The orange won't give any flavour, but works with the apples to keep the duck moist. Close the cavity with butcher's string or meat pins. Rub the skin of the duck very generously with salt and freshly ground black pepper (mix the two together before rubbing), both on the top and underneath.

Preheat the oven to 130°C (275°F) Gas 1.

Pour 500 ml/2 cups water into the roasting pan and place the duck breast-side down on the rack. Roast for an hour, then turn the duck breast-side up for the remaining roasting time of around 3 hours. Baste the duck as you go along, but don't worry too much if the skin isn't crispy, as you will finish it off in the oven at a higher heat. Keep checking the temperature – the duck is done at 72–75°C/161–167°F. The roasting time is not clear cut, as this depends on your oven and the size of the duck, so do check. A good rule is 1¹/₂ hours per 1 kg/2 lb. 4 oz. when roasting at a low temperature. It may need less or more time, but calculate to start your duck around 5–6 hours before you want to serve it, to include resting time. The juices need to run clear when you cut into it, and the bird needs to be cooked through.

Leave the duck for at least 30 minutes to rest, then cut into the legs and breast to get 2–3 pieces from each side. Leave the skin on.

To reheat before serving, pop the duck back into the oven at 120°C (250°F) Gas ¹/₂ for 20–25 minutes to give the skin a chance to crisp up and to heat through before serving. If it needs a bit of help to become crisp, a few minutes under the grill/broiler works.

Serve with gravy made from duck stock (see page 84), Browned Potatoes (see page 81) and Red Cabbage (see page 74).

hasselbackspotatis
HASSELBACK POTATOES

The Hasselback potato is Sweden's answer to the roastie. They first became popular in the 1950s after a trainee chef at Stockholm's Hasselbacken restaurant created them, and are now famous around the world. Hasselback potatoes go well with any kind of roast dinner, and you can vary the flavour by scattering a bit of cheese on top (Parmesan or Västerbottensost work well), or try adding some fresh herbs.

700 g/1 lb. 9 oz. roasting potatoes

oil, for drizzling

50 g/3^{1}/$_{2}$ tablespoons butter

50 g/^{5}/$_{8}$ cup breadcrumbs

salt and freshly ground black pepper

SERVES 4

Preheat the oven to 175°C (350°F) Gas 4.

Peel the potatoes. Take each potato and, using a sharp knife, cut slices two-thirds of the way through at intervals of about 2-3 mm/^{1}/$_{8}$ in. (you can cut very large potatoes in half, if needs be).

Add the potatoes, scored-side up, to an ovenproof dish and drizzle with oil. Season well. Roast in the preheated oven for 25 minutes.

Just before the time is up, melt the butter, then remove the potatoes from the oven. Brush each one with butter over the slices, then sprinkle the breadcrumbs on top. Put the potatoes back in the oven for another 25 minutes or until they're done - the slices will be crispy, and the base of each potato cooked through.

brunede kartofler
BROWNED POTATOES

These Danish caramelized new potatoes are an obligatory side dish on Christmas Eve – they are sweet and delicious with the thick gravy, meat and boiled potatoes. Most people have just a few of them as they are very rich, but they are essential!

1 kg/2 ln. 4 oz. small salad potatoes (I strongly recommend you cook these the day before – see the method)

80 g/6^{1}/$_{2}$ tablespoons caster/superfine sugar

25 g/1^{3}/$_{4}$ tablespoons butter

SERVES 6–8 IF ALSO SERVING BOILED POTATOES

The day before, boil the potatoes until only just done. Take great care not to overcook them, or the final dish will be mushy. I peel off the skin on the potatoes after cooking and cooling – it takes a while, but the result is more pleasant.

About 25 minutes before serving, mix the sugar with 50 ml/3^{1}/$_{2}$ tablespoons water. Heat a frying pan/skillet until it's very hot, then pour in the water-sugar mixture. Let bubble for 3–5 minutes, or until the water has evaporated (the mixture will thicken a bit). Add the butter and let it melt. After 3–4 minutes the mixture will start to turn brown and caramelize. Add the potatoes and swirl them around. Keep the heat high so the caramel remains liquid as you coat the potatoes.

Slowly reduce the heat, bit by bit. The caramel will start to form a thin, sticky layer around the potatoes. The whole process takes around 10–15 minutes from this stage. Keep adjusting the heat to ensure the caramel is fluid enough to stick to the potatoes as you turn them in the pan (the idea is to coat the potatoes with a thin layer of caramel, not end up with a caramel gravy). Serve warm in a bowl.

vegobullar
VEGGIE BALLS

As in many countries, meat-free diets are becoming more popular in Scandinavia. However, these don't always go hand in hand with traditional dishes such as meatballs (see pages 102–103). These 'veggie balls' are my answer to that. They have similar flavour notes to meatballs, and are just as satisfying when served with mash, lingonberries and veggie gravy.

Change the vegetables in this if you like – just as for traditional meatballs, the recipe should become your own. Try swapping carrots for beetroot/beet, celeriac for parsnip, and so on. The nuts can also be changed depending on preference. If you don't have Västerbottensost, use a similar aged cheese such as pecorino or even Parmesan.

1 onion

1 carrot

50 g/2 oz. celeriac

100 g/¾ cup hazelnuts or whole almonds

150 g/1 cup cooked lentils from a jar or can, drained and rinsed

50 g/2 oz. Västerbottensost (or other mature hard cheese), grated

2 eggs

1 teaspoon soy sauce

½ teaspoon ground allspice

½ teaspoon Dijon mustard

2–3 tablespoons freshly chopped parsley

50 g/⅝ cup dried breadcrumbs

2 tablespoons plain/ all-purpose flour

salt and freshly ground black pepper

a glug of oil and a knob of butter, for frying

SERVES 4–5

Place the onion, carrot, celeriac and nuts in a food processor and pulse until chopped. Add the rest of the ingredients (apart from the oil and butter) and pulse again until you have a mixture that can be easily shaped into round balls (a bit larger than a walnut). You should be able to make about 30 veggie balls from the mixture.

Melt the butter and oil in a frying pan/skillet, add a batch of the shaped veggie balls and fry gently until crispy all over. Cook them in batches to avoid overcrowding the pan – if the pan is too full, the balls will steam rather than fry. I usually finish mine in the oven for around 15 minutes on a low heat, which you can do while you're frying the remaining batches.

Note that the water content of the vegetables you use can alter the consistency of the veggie balls – if the balls do not retain their shape during frying, add a little more flour to the mixture.

andesovs

DUCK STOCK GRAVY

This recipe makes the best gravy to accompany the Danish Christmas Roast Duck (see page 78). Some people make gravy from all the liquids in the roasting pan, but I find this a bit too fatty, so I make a duck stock as a base instead.

plain/all-purpose flour

redcurrant jelly (or lingonberry jelly and sugar)

salt

your choice of seasonings, such as gravy browning, soy sauce, Worcestershire sauce, sherry vinegar or cream

FOR THE DUCK STOCK

a knob of butter

a glug of oil

duck giblets and wing tips (from the duck on page 78)

1 carrot, chopped

1 onion, chopped

1/2 leek, chopped

1 parsnip or piece of celeriac, chopped

10 black peppercorns

2–3 allspice berries (optional)

2 whole cloves (optional)

a few sprigs of fresh thyme and parsley

SERVES 4

To make the duck stock, in a saucepan, melt a generous knob of butter and a glug of oil. Add the giblets and the wing tips, then brown really well over a high heat (a darker brown means a darker-coloured gravy). Add your chopped vegetables and spices, then add 1 litre/1 quart water. Leave to simmer, covered, for a few hours until reduced by half, then strain and discard the vegetables, giblets and spices.

Pour the roasting juices from the duck into a clear jug/pitcher. Leave it for a good 30 minutes in the fridge, so the fat starts to separate towards the top of the jug. The longer you leave this, the clearer the separation will be.

In a clean saucepan, heat around 6 tablespoons of duck fat (from the top of the jug/pitcher) until hot, then add 3 tablespoons plain/all-purpose flour to make a roux. You need to have a roux that isn't too liquid or dry, so be ready to add either more fat or flour as needed. Cook the flour to avoid lumps, then add some of your duck stock and stir continuously as the gravy is cooking. You will likely use all of it, but the gravy should still be quite thick. Keep whisking to make sure you end up with a smooth mixture.

Now you can add some of your roasting juices – skim the remaining fat layer off the top of your jug/pitcher and only use the liquid underneath. Keep adding roasting juices, bit by bit, until you have the required thickness of gravy while you boil it. If it's still too thick, add a bit of liquid (from your cooking water, if doing vegetables at the same time).

Add a spoonful of redcurrant or lingonberry jelly and stir. Taste the gravy to see if it needs salt. The gravy might be quite lightly coloured, so a drop of gravy browning works here (or a small drop of soy sauce if you don't have gravy browning). If you find that the gravy tastes of nothing (it sometimes happens), a few drops of Worcestershire sauce and/or sherry vinegar usually does the trick. This is also the point when my mother always adds a squirt of Marmite ('It's the only use I've ever found for Marmite – it makes great gravy!'). A dash of cream adds a decadent final touch.

sovs til flæskesteg
THICK PORK GRAVY

This is the perfect gravy for serving with the Roast Pork on page 70. We eat boiled potatoes not because we like boring food, but because they serve the purpose of soaking up a thick, creamy gravy. If you prefer roast potatoes, by all means serve them – but keep your gravy lighter.

meat juices from the roasting pan (see page 70)

2 tablespoons plain/all-purpose flour

your choice of seasonings, such as salt, freshly ground black pepper, Worcestershire sauce, sugar, sherry

gravy browning (optional)

a glug of cream

SERVES 4

Reserve all the meat juices from the roasting pan in a jug/pitcher and leave to cool. Skim the fat off the top (it will go white and separate from the juices after a few hours in the fridge). Don't discard the fat.

In a saucepan, heat 3 tablespoons of the reserved fat until hot, then add the plain/all-purpose flour to make a roux. Add the stock (the liquid under the fat) and keep boiling and whisking. You may need to add some water, too (the water from boiled potatoes works really well for flavour). Cook until you have your desired thickness of gravy, then taste. You can add more pork fat if it's not fatty enough, or simply season with salt, pepper, Worcestershire sauce, sugar or whatever you like. A drop of sherry or similar adds flavour, too.

Finish with a drop of gravy browning if needed, and a glug of cream. Your finished gravy should be the thickness of double/heavy cream.

rårörda lingon
RAW STIRRED LINGONBERRIES

Lingonberry jam is easily found in Scandinavian shops, but you can also make an easy no-cook version yourself (*rå* means raw in Swedish).

lingonberries

granulated sugar

Simply combine lingonberries with sugar and stir until the sugar dissolves (let them sit at room temperature for a few hours for this to happen). The ratio is usually 2:1 of lingonberries to sugar, but do experiment if you like it more tart or sweet.

This keeps for a week in the fridge, and you can also make it with frozen berries that have been thawed.

THE YULE SMÖRGÅSBORD

In Scandinavia, Christmas Day and Boxing Day are times for visiting extended family and enjoying leisurely lunches full of great food, as well as using up the leftovers from Christmas Eve. These occasions are long and thorough, as we sit around for hours catching up on the year gone by and making plans for the one about to begin.

THREE WAYS WITH HERRING

A Christmas *smörgåsbord* is not complete without pickled herring. At least two kinds are served, always at the beginning of the meal and with a shot of aquavit. Buy a good-quality plain onion herring (such as Danish brand Fiskemandens), drain and dress it in a new flavour, then just wait for a few hours (ideally overnight). Curry herring is Denmark's recipe, while mustard herring is Sweden's favourite and the biggest selling one at ScandiKitchen. It's also a good one to serve to people who don't like the thought of pickled herring. Caviar herring is actually made with roe, but it's the fanciest.

karrysild
CURRY HERRING

100 ml/^{1}/$_3$ cup crème fraîche or sour cream

50 ml/3^1/$_2$ tablespoons mayonnaise

^{1}/$_2$ apple, peeled, cored and finely chopped

1 medium pickled cucumber (around 30 g/1 oz.)

^{1}/$_2$ red onion, finely chopped

1 teaspoon capers, chopped

1 teaspoon mild curry powder

^{1}/$_2$ teaspoon ground turmeric

^{1}/$_2$ teaspoon Dijon mustard

250 g/9 oz. pickled herring (drained weight)

1 tablespoon freshly chopped chives, to garnish (optional)

SERVES 2–3

Mix all the ingredients except the herring in a bowl, then season to taste. Stir in the drained herring and leave to marinate. Garnish with chives, if using. Slices of boiled egg and dark buttered rye bread go well with this.

senapssill
MUSTARD HERRING

1 tablespoon white wine vinegar

3 tablespoons sunflower oil

2 tablespoons crème fraîche or sour cream

2 tablespoons caster/superfine sugar

2 tablespoons Slotts Skånsk Senap (or grain mustard sweetened with a small amount of honey)

1 tablespoon Dijon mustard

2 tablespoons cream

1 tablespoon mayonnaise

1 shallot, very finely chopped

2–3 tablespoons freshly chopped dill

2–3 tablespoons freshly chopped chives

250 g/9 oz. pickled herring (drained weight)

SERVES 2–3

Mix all the ingredients except the herring in a bowl. Whisk until the mixture is creamy and combined, then season to taste. Stir in the drained herring and leave to marinate.

skärgårdssill
CAVIAR HERRING

50 ml/3^1/$_2$ tablespoons mayonnaise

100 ml/^{1}/$_3$ cup crème fraîche or sour cream

3 tablespoons finely chopped chives

3 tablespoons finely chopped dill

^{1}/$_2$ spring onion/scallion, very finely sliced (try to have both white and green bits)

50 g/1^3/$_4$ oz. red lumpfish roe, plus extra to garnish

a squeeze of fresh lemon juice and a bit of grated lemon zest (if you like tangy flavours)

250 g/9 oz. pickled herring (drained weight)

SERVES 2–3

Mix all the ingredients except the herring in a bowl, then season to taste. Stir in the drained herring, then leave to marinate. Serve with extra roe spooned on top.

gravadlax
GRAVLAX

Cured salmon is an essential part of a Christmas *smörgåsbord* in Sweden. It isn't hard to cure your own salmon, it just takes time. To make good gravlax, invest in a good middle piece of salmon fillet, or even a whole side, and leave the skin on. The most important thing is the freshness and quality of the fish, as well as the balance of the curing ingredients used. Dill is the traditional herb to use, but punchy flavours such as fennel and coriander/cilantro also work, or you might even want to try beetroot/beets or red cabbage.

1 kg/2 lb. 4 oz. salmon fillet (a side is usually around 1.3–1.5 kg/2 lb. 14 oz.– 3 lb. 4 oz. – if using a section, go for the middle)

50 g/¼ cup salt

80 g/6½ tablespoons sugar

2 teaspoons white peppercorns, crushed

1 tablespoon gin, vodka or aquavit (optional)

2 bunches of dill (around 60 g/2 oz. in total)

GRAVLAX DRESSING

2 tablespoons Swedish mustard (ideally Slotts Skånsk Senap, otherwise a good Dijon)

4 tablespoons finely chopped dill

1 tablespoon white wine vinegar

1 teaspoon granulated sugar

a pinch of salt and freshly ground black pepper

100 ml/⅓ cup cold-pressed rapeseed/canola or good olive oil

SERVES 10

I always freeze the salmon for 48 hours below -18°C/0°F. Freezing kills most parasites, if any are present, so I think it's good practice to do this. If you buy sushi-grade fish, then it has probably already been frozen (it's a legal requirement in the European Union), but check with your fishmonger. Defrost the salmon in the fridge before using.

Once defrosted, check for bones by running very clean fingers across the fleshy side and using tweezers to pick out any bones you find. Cut the salmon across the middle into two pieces.

Mix together the salt, sugar and white pepper. Rub the alcohol (if using) and a bit of water over the fleshy sides, then rub in the salt, sugar and pepper. Ensure all the flesh is covered.

Chop the dill (including stems) and place on top of one of the flesh sides. Place the other flesh side on top and wrap the fish tightly in clingfilm/plastic wrap. Place the salmon in a plastic bag and place in the fridge. Turn the bag over two or three times a day for the following two or three days to ensure the cure is even. The salmon is ready when the colour of the flesh changes to slightly translucent.

Unwrap the fish and discard the filling (it's fine if a bit of stray dill remains, but it should be mostly clear). Place the salmon flesh-side down and carve into thin slices, cutting through the fish with the knife held at a slight diagonal. Serve with slices of lemon and the gravlax dressing, along with some crispbread or rye bread. The fish will keep for a couple of days, stored in the fridge.

Gravlax dressing
Mix the mustard, dill, vinegar, sugar and salt and pepper in a bowl. Add the oil slowly, starting with a few drops and steadily adding a thin stream to emulsify the sauce. Whisk until you have a good creamy consistency (add a little more oil if too thick).

julskinka
SWEDISH CHRISTMAS HAM

While a ham is the main meat on a Swedish Christmas *smörgåsbord*, most Swedes buy it pre-cooked. In fact, the Swedish *julbord* doesn't have that many cooking components to it, but the sheer volume of different dishes means that just as much planning is required as with any other Yuletide dinner.

It isn't hard to cook your own ham – the trick is only in getting a lightly salted and unsmoked gammon to begin with, and also making sure you use a meat thermometer so it doesn't go dry. Traditionally, Swedish ham is boiled. Some recipes cook it in a pot of water in the oven, others on the hob/stovetop, while other recipes roast it. I prefer boiled and slow-simmered ham to make sure it stays moist. Cook this the day before and add the topping before serving. Swedish ham is served cold, so this is fine (and can even improve the final result).

2.5 kg/5^1/$_2$ lb. lightly salted dry-cured unsmoked gammon, with some fat on

1 onion, quartered

10 black peppercorns

2–3 bay leaves

salt

MUSTARD TOPPING

1 egg yolk

3 heaped tablespoons grainy Swedish mustard

3 heaped tablespoons breadcrumbs

meat thermometer

SERVES 8–10 AS PART OF A CHRISTMAS *JULBORD*

Place the ham in a large saucepan, cover water, add the onion, peppercorns and bay leaves and bring to the boil. Skim off any fat that rises to the top of the water.

Reduce to a very slow simmer and cover with a lid. The cooking time depends on the thickness and size of the meat. A rule of thumb is 45–50 minutes per 1 kg/2 lb. 4 oz., but when the temperature in the middle reaches 72°C (162°F), it is done. If you have a longer, thinner piece, it will be ready faster than a very fat, rounder piece. Always use your common sense and a meat thermometer.

Remove the ham from the water and leave to cool. I usually cover it with clingfilm/plastic wrap to prevent the outside from going dry.

To prepare for the topping before serving, preheat the oven to 200°C (400°F) Gas 6. Trim off the fat from the top of the cooked ham and tidy it up a bit. Mix the ingredients for the mustard topping with a fork and simply spread over the top of the ham (use your hands). Put the ham into the preheated oven to allow the topping to bake – you may need to pop it under a hot grill/broiler at the end, too. The topping needs to set around the ham to give a mustard crust.

Serve whole on the Christmas table and slice as needed. Leftover ham makes an amazing carbonara sauce for pasta, or make ham and Västerbottensost cheese rye bread toasties.

rødkålssalat
RED CABBAGE SALAD

Not everyone likes cooked cabbage with Christmas dinner, so I often make this fresh and tangy salad to serve alongside the heavy meats and other side dishes. It's so simple, but still tastes very Christmassy.

500 g/1 lb. 2 oz. red cabbage

1 small red onion

5 tablespoons olive oil

3 tablespoons white wine vinegar

1 tablespoon balsamic vinegar

freshly squeezed juice of 1 orange

1 tablespoon granulated sugar

1 teaspoon Dijon mustard

1 teaspoon salt flakes

2 ripe Conference pears

100 g/1 cup walnut pieces

salt and freshly ground black pepper

SERVES 6 AS A GENEROUS SIDE DISH

Finely slice the cabbage and red onion and place in a bowl. Mix together the remaining ingredients (apart from the pears and walnuts), then pour over the red cabbage and onion and toss. Set aside for a few hours to allow the flavours to mingle. This will also soften the cabbage and onion.

Just before serving, core and finely slice the pears and toast the walnuts. Mix with the cabbage and serve.

Variations
Swap the walnuts for toasted pumpkin seeds. For an even fresher taste, add finely chopped flat-leaf parsley and fold in.

You can also make this as a salad to serve on its own, crumbling in either a good goats' cheese or some blue cheese. Adding a few rye bread croutons also works.

agurkesalat
PICKLED CUCUMBER

This is the side dish that goes with everything. Perfect on a *smörgåsbord*, as a final topping for an open sandwich, in a meatball dinner (see page 102) – there are so many uses. I make a batch of this every week – it's fresher than proper pickled cucumbers and nicely crunchy. For a variation, you can also make this with thinly sliced red onion.

2 cucumbers

120 g/^{1}/$_2$ cup caster/granulated sugar

200 ml/^{3}/$_4$ cup white wine vinegar

3–4 tablespoons finely chopped dill

salt and freshly ground black pepper

SERVES 4

Slice the cucumber thinly (a mandoline works well) and place in a bowl. Add several teaspoons of salt and leave for around 30 minutes.

In a saucepan, bring the sugar, vinegar and 200 ml/^{3}/$_4$ cup water to a simmer. When the sugar has dissolved, take off the heat and season generously.

Rinse the cucumbers to remove the salt, then add to the liquid. If they taste too sour, add more sugar. If they're too sweet, add a dash of vinegar. Add the dill, then leave to rest for a minimum of 30 minutes before eating. Serve in the liquid.

Keeps for at least 4–5 days in the fridge.

grønkålssalát
QUICK KALE SALAD

Most kale in Scandinavian recipes is cooked, but I prefer the tarter bite of fresh curly kale. If you spend 5 minutes massaging the kale (yes, you read right) the bitterness disappears and you end up with a silky, beautiful bitter-on-the-bite salad, perfect next to rich meats.

75 g/generous ½ cup hazelnuts

200 g/7 oz. curly kale

at least 3 tablespoons freshly squeezed lemon juice

2 heads of chicory/endive

2 tart apples

seeds from ½ a pomegranate

olive oil and seasoning, as needed

SERVES 3

Toast the hazelnuts in a hot pan and set aside to cool. Remove and discard the stalks from the kale, and chop the leaves roughly.

In a bowl, combine the lemon juice and a pinch of salt, then add the kale. Massage with your fingers for about 5 minutes – you will see the kale changing colour to a deeper green, and it will also feel softer. This means the harsh bitterness will also disappear.

Discard the outer layers of the chicory/endive leaves, then thinly slice and add to the salad. Core and chop the apples and add to the bowl. Hold the pomegranate half over the bowl, cut-side down, and beat out the seeds using a wooden spoon.

Raw kale salad doesn't need a lot of dressing – mainly just the lemon. I usually just add a glug of olive oil and check if it needs more lemon and salt. If it's too tangy, a pinch of sugar or even runny honey works, but don't use any creamy dressings. Taste and season as preferred. Finally, fold in the hazelnuts and serve.

grønlangkål
JUTLANDIC STEWED KALE

This is a *husmanskost* recipe from the Jutland region of Denmark. *Husmanskost* is a word used to describe traditional, hearty, filling food. Blanched kale in white sauce is a Christmas favourite and works well with pork and ham. It isn't the prettiest of dishes, but this wouldn't be an inclusive Scandinavian Christmas book without it. As well as Jutland, *grønlangkål* is popular elsewhere in Denmark, southern Sweden and northern Germany. Leftovers make a good base for a quiche.

650 g/1 lb. 7 oz. curly kale

25 g/1¾ tablespoons butter

25 g/3 tablespoons plain/all-purpose flour

300 ml/1¼ cups milk (or a mix of half milk and half cream)

salt and freshly ground black pepper

mustard, sugar or vinegar (optional)

SERVES 4

Remove the stalks from the kale and chop the leaves finely. Blanch in water for 7–8 minutes – if you have water from cooking ham or other meat, it works well for flavour. Drain.

In a saucepan, melt the butter and add the flour to make a roux. Whisk well, then start to add the milk, bit by bit. The usual rule is that the more special the occasion, the more cream is used, so the ratio is up to you and the occasion.

Add the kale to the sauce and leave to stew for several minutes over a low heat. Season with salt and pepper (and maybe a small bit of mustard), to taste. The kale, depending on how bitter it is, might also need a bit of sugar or a drop of vinegar. Use your own judgement.

Janssons frestelse
JANSSON'S TEMPTATION

An essential on any Swedish Christmas table, the humble Jansson's Temptation is actually one of the stars. It is one of the most misunderstood dishes outside Sweden because it includes *ansjovis*, often mistranslated into English as 'anchovies'. Swedish *ansjovis* are a sweet, pickled sprat; if you use the salty Italian anchovies found on a pizza, the taste will not be authentic. The most famous brand of sprat used for this is Grebbestads ansjovis original, which we sell in our shop and online. Your local IKEA may also stock it. If you cannot find this brand, try finely chopped pickled herring instead.

700 g/1 lb. 9 oz. floury potatoes (such as Russet, King Edward or Maris Piper)

25 g/1¾ tablespoons butter

200 g/7 oz. sliced white onions

125-g/4½-oz. can of *ansjovis* (see introduction) or finely chopped pickled herring

300 ml/1¼ cups whole milk

300 ml/1¼ cups double/heavy cream

3–4 tablespoons dried breadcrumbs

salt and freshly ground black pepper

ovenproof dish approx. 30 x 15-cm/12 x 6-in.

SERVES 4 AS A SIDE

Preheat the oven to 180°C (350°F) Gas 4.

Peel the potatoes and cut into matchsticks, a little thinner than French fries. Do this in one go and don't soak them in water as you want to keep the starch. Put the potatoes in an ovenproof dish and place in the preheated oven for around 20 minutes to pre-cook them a bit.

Meanwhile, melt the butter in a saucepan and add the sliced onions. Cook over a gentle heat until soft, taking care not to brown them. Remove the potatoes from the oven and add to the onions, mixing gently without breaking them up, and fold together.

Place half the potatoes and onion back in the ovenproof dish. Place half the *ansjovis* over the vegetables and season well. Mix the milk and cream together, then pour half the mixture over the vegetables in the dish.

Repeat with another layer of the potatoes and *ansjovis*, pour over the rest of the milk and cream and finish with a scattering of breadcrumbs on top. The cream and milk mixture should reach the top of the dish.

Pop back in the oven and bake for around 30–35 minutes or until the potatoes are cooked through. Some potatoes soak up more liquid than others, so you may need to add more milk and cream during cooking – you want the end result to be creamy.

Variation
Omit the *ansjovis* and this becomes a lovely vegetarian potato gratin. If you do this, I suggest you add a few drops of white wine vinegar to the milk and cream mixture and adjust the seasoning. If you want a bit of a bite, add some capers.

the Christmas Table

Every year, my mother worries if there is enough food for Christmas Eve. We've never been short of anything, but she still worries. Since I started to host Christmas myself, I find myself worrying as well, so it must be a family trait.

On Christmas Day, the fridge door can still hardly close, so making sure we get through all the food means more parties and spending extra time with people we love. That's not a bad thing, of course – except perhaps for our waistlines.

The two days after Christmas Eve are the time to visit extended family, eat even more, and continue the celebrations. In Denmark, it is not unusual to visit one side of the family on Christmas Day, and the other on Boxing Day. By the time the 27th rolls in, we generally can't move and will become at one with the sofa for the 'in-between days' until New Year.

A Christmas *smörgåsbord* is enjoyed by Swedes as their main Christmas Eve meal and is called a *julbord*. Danes and some Norwegians also follow suit in the days after. The *julbord* is a serious business and can take a long time to enjoy. In my home, it is not unusual for such an occasion to take up to 6–7 hours of sitting around, eating, drinking and chatting. In the days before Christmas, most companies lay on a *julbord* for their employees, and people host them for friends. It is a huge part of our Yuletide.

In all Scandinavian countries, a *smörgåsbord* starts with pickled herring, usually served on a separate plate. Herring is the strongest flavour

in the meal, and can overpower the rest of the dishes if served later on. To toast the herring, most people enjoy a shot (or several) of aquavit, a very strong grain-based spirit that tends to get people intoxicated from the waist down, then up. As aquavit is usually enjoyed 'down in one', most non-Scandinavian guests are warned to pace themselves. Few listen.

The second round of this feast brings other fish dishes. Cured salmon, fried plaice fillets, smoked salmon, mackerel, prawns/shrimp and pâtés – all the fish arrive in small dishes so everybody can have a little taste. With many more courses to come, less is more, so we can always spot a rookie if they're filling up their plate at this stage.

Round three is usually cold sliced meats (salami, liver pâté, cold salt beef or roast beef), followed

by round four: the warm meats, featuring meatballs and warm pork. In Sweden, this is where the ham and Jansson's Temptation arrive on the *julbord*. Cheese is usually reserved for the fifth round.

Finally, if there is space, creamed rice pudding is brought to the table, followed by cookies and marzipan treats with coffee. Different varieties of breads are served throughout, along with beetroot/beet salad and other sides, so people can choose lighter options if they prefer.

It's hard to imagine how we can eat all this food and still function, but as with everything in Scandinavia, balance is key. Serving sizes are small and people are sitting down for many hours, enjoying the food slowly. Quite often, the lunch is followed by a long walk (or even preceded by one). The real purpose of a *smörgåsbord* is never just to eat – the intention is to connect with each other and really talk. It is a wonderful time for Christmas *hygge* with no distractions.

THE THREE MEATBALLS

medisterkaker

NORWEGIAN MEATBALLS

It is impossible to write a Scandinavian Christmas book without our three meatball recipes. If I were to only add one of them, there would be uproar from the two countries that were missing. So, you get all three, and I keep the peace between Sweden, Denmark and Norway.

Scandinavia is a huge place and our meatball recipes vary by region, as well as by country. I've included the most significant variations and descriptions here, but even so, there are so many further types. Meatballs are perfected by each individual who cooks them, so use my recipes as a guide from which to create your own.

Despite the differences, all the variations are usually served with potatoes (see page 81), brown gravy and some form of red cabbage (see page 74) or lingonberries (see page 85) all year round, not just at Christmas. Each batch serves four for dinner, but one batch is sufficient as a side dish for a large gathering.

Tip for Swedish meatballs: if they do not retain their round shape, add a small amount of fine breadcrumbs to your hands before rolling. This will help to crisp up the outside, but don't overdo the crumbs as they can be a bit drying.

These are served alongside traditional Norwegian Christmas Eve food such as *ribbe* (see page 70). There are two kinds of meatballs in Norway. Some are called *kjøttkaker*, made with beef, while the ones here are known as *medisterkaker* and use pork. At Christmas time, *medisterkaker* are more likely to be served.

500 g/1 lb. 2 oz. minced/ground pork (minimum 15% fat)

2 teaspoons salt

2 teaspoons plain/all-purpose flour

1 egg

1/4 teaspoon ground ginger

1/2 teaspoon ground nutmeg

1/2 teaspoon ground white pepper

100 ml/1/3 cup whole milk

butter or fat, for frying (if you're making *ribbe*, use some of its fat for flavour)

MAKES 8-10

In a stand mixer, mix the pork and salt for a few minutes with a paddle attachment, then add all the other ingredients except the milk. You need a good, firm texture, so you might not need the milk at all. If you do, gradually add it a little at a time until the mixture is firm.

Wet your hands, then use a tablespoon to scoop out some meat mixture about half the size of a burger patty. Use the flat of your hand and the spoon to help form the meatballs into a slight oval shape.

Heat the butter or fat in a frying pan/skillet, then add the meatballs to the pan, flattening them down to around 1.5 cm/5/8 in. in height (don't crowd the pan). Fry for around 5 minutes on each side until browned, then transfer to a warm oven until you are ready to serve.

köttbullar
SWEDISH MEATBALLS

The meatball is one of Sweden's biggest exports, but the homemade version is a far cry from the supermarket varieties. This is a great recipe which you can adjust to make your own. Leftovers are great in sandwiches with some Beetroot Salad (see page 106).

30 g/$^1/_2$ cup dried breadcrumbs (or oats if you prefer)

150 ml/$^2/_3$ cup chicken stock

400 g/14 oz. minced/ ground beef

200 g/7 oz. minced/ ground pork (minimum 10% fat)

1 teaspoon salt

1 small onion, grated (squeeze out any excess juice)

1 egg

2$^1/_2$ tablespoons plain/ all-purpose flour

1 teaspoon ground allspice

1 teaspoon ready-made mustard

$^1/_2$ teaspoon ground white pepper

$^1/_2$ teaspoon freshly ground black pepper

a dash of Worcestershire Sauce, soy sauce or Marmite

butter and oil, for frying

MAKES 30–40

Soak the breadcrumbs in the stock and set aside. In a stand mixer, combine the meats with the salt for a good few minutes. Add the onion, egg, flour, allspice and breadcrumb mixture and mix until everything is combined to a reasonably firm mixture. Add the remaining ingredients, then set aside to rest in a cold place for 30 minutes.

With wet hands, form a small meatball the size of a walnut – this is your test ball. Melt the butter with oil in a frying pan/skillet until browned, then fry the meatball for a few minutes until cooked all the way through. Taste, then adjust the seasoning as needed, then test another one.

Again, with wet hands, roll the remaining meatballs. Don't fry too many at once or they'll lump together – once done, keep them warm in the oven while you finish the rest.

frikadeller
DANISH MEATBALLS

The Danish version of meatballs is eaten hot or cold at a Christmas or *smörgåsbord* lunch, but funnily enough they never make an appearance on Christmas Eve.

300 g/10$^1/_2$ oz. minced/ ground veal

200 g/7 oz. minced/ ground pork

1 teaspoon salt

1 onion, grated (squeeze out any excess juice)

1 egg

3 tablespoons breadcrumbs

1 tablespoon plain/ all-purpose flour

1 teaspoon ground allspice (optional)

a pinch of ground nutmeg (optional)

100 ml/$^1/_3$ cup warm milk, with $^1/_2$ stock cube dissolved in it

freshly ground black pepper

100 ml/$^1/_3$ cup plus 1 tablespoon sparkling water

75 g/5 tablespoons butter and a glug of oil, for frying

MAKES 10–12

In a stand mixer, add the meat and salt and mix for about a minute. Add the onion to the mixer along with all the other ingredients, except the water. Mix thoroughly, then rest for at least 30 minutes in a cold place.

Add the sparkling water to the meat mixture and stir by hand to combine.

In a frying pan/skillet, heat the butter and leave it to brown and bubble, then add a glug of oil.

Wet your hands, then use the method opposite for the Norwegian version, making meatballs the size of large eggs. Fry for 2–3 minutes on each side, then keep warm in the oven to finish cooking until you're ready to serve.

rødbedesalat
BEETROOT SALAD

Over the past decade of running ScandiKitchen, this is the recipe I have shared most often. We make so much of this salad every day. It's delicious, versatile and indulgent while still being good for you. Every Scandinavian Christmas lunch features a variation of it. In Denmark, my aunt Vibeke's recipe includes whipped cream. In Sweden, my father-in-law Leif's version features pickled cucumber. My own recipe makes enough for six people as a side, and maybe with leftovers to add to meatball sandwiches.

2 jars of pickled beetroot/beets, to give you around 600 g/1 lb. 5 oz. of beetroot/beets once drained*

sugar, if needed

1 tart apple (Granny Smith or similar)

a squeeze of fresh lemon juice

75 g/$^1/_3$ cup mayonnaise

100 g/$^1/_2$ cup crème fraîche or sour cream

2–3 tablespoons balsamic vinegar

salt and freshly ground black pepper

SERVES 6 AS A SIDE

* Not all pickled beetroot/beets taste the same. Scandinavian brands have a sweet brine, despite no sweeteners being used (I prefer the Felix and Beauvais brands). In some countries sweeteners are used, but avoid these if you can. Eastern European versions tend to be a bit sourer, so you might need to add a bit of sugar. You do need sweetness in this salad.

Drain the beetroot/beets, then dice into cubes no larger than 1 cm/$^1/_2$ in. Taste to see if it needs sugar – if so, sprinkle a little on top of the beetroot/beets (around 1–2 tablespoons, according to taste).

Peel and core the apple, then cube to the same size as the beetroot. Squeeze the lemon juice over the apple cubes.

To make the dressing, mix the mayonnaise and crème fraîche or sour cream with the balsamic vinegar, salt and pepper.

Mix the beetroot/beets and apple together, then mix with the dressing. It will appear quite pink at this point, but will go darker after a few hours in the fridge as the juices penetrate the dressing. You can always add a dollop of mayo just before serving if you feel it has gone too dark – aim for a bright, deep pink.

Ways to pimp your beetroot
- Leif's way: add chopped pickled cucumber or gherkins.
- Vibeke's way: just before serving, fold in a few spoonfuls of whipped cream (no sugar added).
- Add chopped capers.
- If you want a herring side salad for a smörgåsbord, mix a few chopped hard-boiled/cooked eggs with chopped pickled herring fillets and beetroot salad to taste.
- Cube cooked carrot and potato and add to the beetroot along with red onions and capers to create what Danes call a 'Russian salad'.
- Replace the mayo with skyr or quark to keep the dish lighter.
- Add toasted, chopped walnuts for a nutty finish.
- Add a handful of chopped chives and some chopped dried apricots (soak them for an hour first to plump them up).
- Swap the mayo and crème fraîche for crumbled feta and toasted hazelnuts. Add dill if you like. (This version is pictured right.)

CHRISTMAS BREADS

Healthier dark rye and crispbread may dominate at other
times of the year, but Christmas is the season for treating
ourselves with sweeter breads and family recipes
handed down by our mothers
and grandmothers.

vörtbröd

SWEDISH CHRISTMAS BREAD

At Christmas time, this bread is hugely popular in Sweden – it is a sweet loaf served on the *smörgåsbord* with the ham (see page 92). There are raisins in *vörtbröd*, but you can leave them out if you prefer a less sweet finish (this bread is sold with and without in Sweden). Ground bitter orange peel can be hard to find (and hard to grind), but you can get it in Nordic food shops and, of course, online. If you can only get whole peel, use a spice grinder or clean coffee grinder to pulverize it.

50 g/3^1/$_2$ tablespoons butter, plus extra for brushing

1 teaspoon ground dried bitter orange peel

1 tablespoon ground ginger

1^1/$_2$ teaspoons ground cloves

1 teaspoon ground cardamom

25 g/^{7}/$_8$ oz. fresh yeast

250 ml/1 cup Guinness (or a similar stout)

80 ml/^{1}/$_3$ cup black treacle/molasses

2 tablespoons malt extract

200 g/scant 2 cups wholegrain rye flour

1 tablespoon sea salt

500 g/3^1/$_2$ cups white strong bread flour

100 g/^{3}/$_4$ cup raisins (optional)

MAKES 2 LOAVES

Melt the butter, stir in the ground orange peel, ginger, cloves and cardamom, and leave to infuse.

In a stand mixer, add the yeast and 250 ml/1 cup lukewarm water (no warmer than 37°C/98°F) and stir to dissolve. Add the stout and treacle/molasses, then mix again. Add the butter-spice mix and malt extract, then start to add the flour: begin with the rye, then add the salt. Continue with the white flour. If using, stir in the raisins as you add the white flour. You need to add enough flour to have a sticky, firm dough – you may need more or less flour than specified here.

Leave the dough to rise in a warm place for at least an hour or until doubled in size. You can also prove it for longer in a colder place.

Knead and shape into two loaves, place on a baking sheet, then leave to rise under cover for another hour.

Preheat the oven to 240°C (475°F) Gas 9. Fill a small ovenproof bowl with water and leave to one side.

Melt a small amount of butter and brush the tops of the loaves. Place them in the preheated oven and turn the temperature down to 200°C (400°F) Gas 6, then place the bowl of water in the bottom of the oven, closing the door immediately after. This will help a crust to form.

Bake for around 30 minutes until golden and done. The bread is ready when the internal temperature reaches 98°C/208°F. Baking times vary by oven, so if the bread is going too dark during baking, you may need to reduce the heat a little.

britiske juleboller

MINCEMEAT BUNS

The secret to a soft, fragrant cinnamon bun is in the dough, but there's a twist here – my Norwegian colleague Martina uses mincemeat (non-British readers: don't be scared, it's a traditional sweet fruit filling, available online). It works really well, but if you want to stick to Scandi traditions, use the cinnamon filling.

BASIC BUN DOUGH

250 ml/1 cup whole milk, heated to 36–37°C/97–98°F

25 g/⁷/₈ oz. fresh yeast

80 g/5¹/₂ tablespoons butter, melted and cooled slightly

40 g/3¹/₄ tablespoons caster/superfine sugar

400–500 g/3–3¹/₂ cups white strong bread flour

2 teaspoons ground cardamom

1 teaspoon salt

1 egg, beaten

FILLING

400-g/14-oz. shop-bought jar of mincemeat

FOR BRUSHING

beaten egg (the remaining half)

100 g/¹/₂ cup sugar (for the sugar syrup)

pearl/nibbed sugar (optional)

CINNAMON FILLING (OPTIONAL)

100 g/7 tablespoons soft butter

100 g/¹/₂ cup sugar (I use half soft brown, half white)

1 tablespoon ground cinnamon

¹/₂ teaspoon vanilla extract

1 teaspoon plain/all-purpose flour

MAKES 16

To make the bun dough, put the warm milk into the bowl of a stand mixer, add the yeast and stir until dissolved. Add the cooled, melted butter. Allow to combine with the yeast for a minute or so, then add the sugar and leave for another minute.

Place 400 g/3 cups of the flour in another bowl. Mix in the cardamom and salt. Start adding the flour mixture into the milk bit by bit. Add half the beaten egg and knead for 5 minutes. You may need to add more flour to get a dough that's a bit sticky, but not so much that it sticks to your finger if you poke it. It's better not to add too much flour as this will result in dry buns – you can always add more later.

Leave the dough in the bowl in a warm place, covered with a tea towel/ dish towel or clingfilm/plastic wrap. Allow to rise for around 30 minutes or until doubled in size. Dust your work surface with flour and turn the dough onto it. Using your hands, knead the dough and work in more flour if needed, then roll it out to a 40 x 50-cm/16 x 20-in. rectangle.

Spread the mincemeat across the dough in a thin, even layer. You may have some left over, but keep the layer thin. Roll the dough lengthways into a long roll and slice into 16 pieces. Place on a baking sheet lined with baking parchment, cover and leave to rise for another 20 minutes.

Preheat the oven to 200°C (400°F) Gas 6.

Brush the buns lightly with beaten egg, then bake for 6–9 minutes, or until golden and done. They can burn easily, so keep an eye on them.

To make the sugar syrup, in a pan heat 50 ml/3¹/₂ tablespoons water with the sugar until bubbling and melted. When the buns come out of the oven, immediately brush lightly with the syrup, then scatter over pearl/nibbed sugar, if using. Cover with a damp tea towel/dish towel to stop them going dry and leave to cool.

Variation
For cinnamon buns, mix the filling ingredients together until smooth and spread onto the rolled-out dough. Proceed as above.

hönökaka

SWEDISH SOFT FLATBREAD

The Swedish *hönökaka* is named after the island of Hönö, off the coast of Gothenburg, where it was originally baked by fishing and farming families. Shop-bought *hönökakor* are common in Sweden, but can be a bit sweet. I use light brown sugar, but not as much as in other recipes – I find it gives a rounded taste to the bread. I make a few of these weekly for the kids' lunchboxes, and as a bread for a *smörgåsbord*. It also goes really well as a sandwich bread with fish and seafood. I prefer a plain *hönökako*, but you can add fennel or caraway seeds, or whatever else you might like.

50 g/2 oz. fresh yeast

50 g/¼ cup soft light brown sugar

400 g/4 scant cups white rye flour

400 g/3 cups white strong bread flour, plus extra for dusting (you may not use all of either flour, so use them equally as you go)

1 tablespoon salt

100 g/7 tablespoons butter, at room temperature

MAKES 6 LARGE BREADS (THEY FREEZE REALLY WELL)

Dissolve the fresh yeast in 500 ml/2 cups lukewarm water in the bowl of a stand mixer. Mix for a minute or so, then add the sugar and mix again to dissolve. Add two-thirds of each of the two flours, plus all the salt, and start mixing. You may not need all the flour, which is why you start with the amount indicated, then add more of each as you need it. Add the butter and keep mixing until it is incorporated. Add more of the flours as needed. When the dough starts letting go of the sides of the bowl (after around 5 minutes of kneading in the machine and with enough flour added), cover the dough and leave to rest in a warm place for around an hour, or until it has doubled in size.

Turn the dough out onto a floured surface and knead, then cut it into six equal-sized pieces. Roll each one out to a circle with a diameter of 30 cm/12 in., then prick all over with a fork and place on baking parchment. Leave to rise again under a tea towel/dish towel for around 40 minutes.

Preheat the oven to 240°C (475°F) Gas 9. I add the baking sheets to the oven at this stage, as placing the *hönökakor* on a hot sheet speeds up the baking on the underside of the bread – much the same as using a pizza stone to make a base.

Prick again with the fork just before you pop the bread into the oven (you may need to bake them in batches). Bake for around 8 minutes, but keep an eye on them, as they can go brown quickly due to the sugar content. You want them slightly golden, but not overly brown.

Remove from the oven and leave to cool under a damp tea towel/dish towel while you bake the rest of the breads.

sötlimpa

SWEDISH SWEET LOAF

Swedes mostly eat crispbread, but they also love sweetened breads like this one. The end result isn't as sweet as you'd expect, but the sugars are important for taste and texture, as well as the proving. I adore this bread almost straight out of the oven with a good strong cheese! You can bake in pans or freehand. This recipe makes two large loaves, but if you wish to make three smaller ones, reduce your baking time accordingly. If proving overnight, you can reduce the yeast by at least half and leave, covered, to rise in a room of around 12–14°C (54–57°F) for 12 hours.

50 g/1³/₄ oz. fresh yeast

100 g/¹/₂ cup soft dark brown sugar

75 g/¹/₄ cup golden/corn syrup

50 g/3¹/₂ tablespoons butter, melted and cooled slightly

100 ml/¹/₃ cup soured dairy product, such as buttermilk

450 g/3¹/₄ cups white strong bread flour, plus extra for dusting

400 g/scant 4 cups white rye flour

100 g/³/₄ cup wholemeal/whole-wheat rye flour

1 heaped teaspoon salt

1 egg

beaten egg or oil, for brushing

MAKES 2 LOAVES

In a stand mixer, add the fresh yeast and 500 ml/2 cups lukewarm water (no warmer than 37°C/98°F), and stir to dissolve for a minute or so. Add the sugar and syrup and keep mixing for another minute or so, then add the melted butter and soured dairy product. Start adding the flour bit by bit, along with the salt and egg.

Keep adding the flour and knead the dough for around 5 minutes. The dough should be stretchy, but not dry. You may not need all the flour, so reserve any remainder for the second kneading.

Cover the bowl with clingfilm/plastic wrap and leave to rise in a warm place for about an hour until the dough has doubled in size.

Turn out onto a floured surface and knead the dough with your hands for a few minutes. Cut into two pieces, then shape into loaves or place in loaf pans. Leave to rise again for 40 minutes.

Preheat the oven to 220°C (425°F) Gas 7.

Brush the surface of the loaves with beaten egg or oil. Place in the preheated oven, then immediately reduce the heat to 200°C (400°F) Gas 6. The baking time is around 30-40 minutes, or until baked through. Watch the surface of the bread - if it goes brown too quickly, reduce the heat a little.

Remove from the oven, cover with a damp tea towel/dish towel to prevent a crust forming and leave to cool.

skorpor

CARDAMOM RUSKS

If I'm ever peckish before bed (quite often, really), I reach for crispy rusks like these *skorpor*. They're a great snack at any time of the day, but when you need a little something and you're trying to avoid the chocolate bar in the cupboard, they're perfect. The addition of the cardamom gives them a lovely flavour, too.

Skorpor can be made with either yeast or baking powder. This recipe takes the baking powder route, simply because it is super-easy. The secret to good *skorpor* is to ensure they are entirely dried out, so use the baking times as a guide. Sometimes I just leave them in the oven overnight after baking (with the oven turned off) so they're completely dry the next day.

100 g/7 tablespoons butter, softened

50 g/¼ cup soft light brown sugar

400 g/3 cups white strong bread flour

100 g/¾ cup wholemeal/whole-wheat flour

2 teaspoons ground cardamom

2 teaspoons baking powder

1 egg

200 ml/¾ cup milk

½ teaspoon salt

MAKES APPROX. 40

Preheat the oven to 220°C (425°F) Gas 7. Line a couple of baking sheets with baking parchment.

Cream the butter and sugar in the bowl of a stand mixer, then add all the remaining ingredients and mix until you have a sticky dough. You may need a bit of extra flour.

Roll the dough into egg-sized balls, then transfer to the baking sheets. Place them in the preheated oven and bake for 10 minutes. Remove from the oven, then, using a fork or knife, carefully slice them in half. Lie them cut-side up on the lined baking sheets.

Reduce the oven temperature to 180°C (350°F) Gas 4 and put the *skorpor* back in for another 15–20 minutes for an even bake. Depending on your oven, the *skorpor* may need less or more baking time to be completely dry and baked through for a very crispy result.

Leave until completely crisp and dry, and enjoy with butter, jam/preserves, cheese or whatever you fancy.

julekringle
CHRISTMAS KRINGLE

Kringle is a Scandinavian word for pretzel. While the traditional shape is the same as the well-known German variety, I'm calling these *kringle* because the recipe is the same as the one used for Danish pastries. Every Scandinavian bakery has a *kringle* sign outside the door – while the *kringle* might not be in the traditional shape, it will still usually be filled with dried fruit, marzipan and nuts. This dough is the basis of all *wienerbrød*, or what we call Danish pastries in Denmark. It is a flaky, deliciously sweet pastry, and while it does take a little time and practice, it isn't difficult. Tasting these treats straight from the oven more than makes up for the effort. You can use this dough as a base for other Danish treats such as swirls, *spandauer* and *tebirkes*.

25 g/⁷/₈ oz. fresh yeast
150 ml/²/₃ cup whole milk, finger warm (not hot)
50 g/¹/₄ cup sugar
50 g/3¹/₂ tablespoons unsalted butter, softened
1 teaspoon salt
350 g/2¹/₂ cups white strong bread flour, plus extra for dusting
1 egg and 1 egg yolk

BUTTER LAYER
350 g/3 sticks unsalted butter
25 g/3 tablespoons plain/all-purpose flour

ALMOND PASTE
100 g/¹/₃ cup marzipan (minimum 50% almonds)
100 g/7 tablespoons butter, softened
100 g/³/₄ cup icing/confectioners' sugar

FILLING FOR 2 KRINGLER
100 g/³/₄ cup raisins, soaked overnight in Amaretto
50 g/⁵/₈ cup flaked/slivered almonds
pearl/nibbed sugar or light icing, to decorate (optional)

MAKES 2

In a stand mixer bowl, dissolve the fresh yeast in the milk. Add the sugar and softened butter, then stir again. Add the salt to the flour and start to add, bit by bit. About halfway through adding the flour, add the whole egg, then continue to add the flour. Keep mixing for at least 5 minutes until the dough is a bit sticky. You may not need all the flour, or you could require a little more – just make sure the dough isn't dry.

Cover the bowl with clingfilm/plastic wrap and leave to rise in a warm place for about an hour.

Turn the dough out onto a floured surface and knead, adding more flour as needed to make it stretchy and workable. Roll the dough out into a big square approx. 35 x 35 cm/14 x 14 in., as evenly as you can.

To make the butter layer, using your hands, form the butter with the flour into a ball that's just mouldable with a rolling pin. It's important that the butter ends up being of a similar consistency to the dough, as it will make it easier to roll. If your hands are too warm, use a rolling pin to beat the butter flat. Flatten out to a square of approx. 25 x 25 cm/ 10 x 10 in. Place the butter square on top of your dough, but shifted at a 45-degree angle, so the dough corners can fold back in to cover the butter like an envelope.

Carefully fold the dough corners over the butter until you have completely enclosed the butter. Dust with some flour, then carefully roll out the package to a rectangle of around 30 x 50cm/12 x 20 in. Fold in the layers the short way twice, so you end up with a rectangle of approximately 30 x 15 cm/12 x 6 in. (three layers with butter).

Continued overleaf

Continued from
previous page

It is very important that you roll carefully over the dough so the butter stays inside the package. Rest the dough for 15 minutes on a baking sheet in the fridge – it's important you do this in the fridge so it doesn't rise and the butter is kept cold. Remove from the fridge to repeat the process: roll to a rectangle and fold back on itself so you now have nine layers of butter. Rest the dough in the fridge again.

Repeat for a final time so you end up with yet another rectangle in three folds – and now 27 layers of butter. After a further little fridge rest, your pastry is ready to shape into whatever you want to bake.

At any stage during the making of Danish pastries, if your hands or the dough get too warm, cool your hands in cold water, as the heat can spoil the end result.

Line two baking sheets with baking parchment. Carefully roll out the dough, taking care not to break the butter layers. Roll until you have a piece approx. 35-cm/14-in. wide and 40–45 cm/16–18 in. long (it will be quite thin). Cut down the middle lengthways so you are left with two rectangular pieces.

To make the almond paste, grate the marzipan into a bowl. Add the softened butter and sugar. Mix everything together until smooth and it is ready to use.

Add the almond paste down the middle of each piece of dough (leaving the sides clear), then add the raisins. Carefully fold each side of the dough into the middle, covering the raisins and marzipan but not overlapping the dough, and press down to make it stick. You want the dough edges to meet but not overlap. Carefully transfer to the lined baking sheets. Leave to prove for at least another 30 minutes, then brush with the egg yolk and scatter over the almonds and pearl/nibbed sugar, if using.

Preheat the oven to 200°C (400°F) Gas 6.

Place the *kringler* in the preheated oven and bake for 20–30 minutes until done. You will get some leaking out of butter – this is normal and it's best to place another baking sheet in the bottom of the oven to catch the melted butter. Keep an eye on the *kringler* and if the tops of the pastry go too dark, cover with foil.

Variation
If you don't want to make two *kringler*, you can bake one and freeze the other half of the dough. Alternatively, use the second half of the dough to make Danish pastries. These will bake in about 10 minutes.

hurtigt rugbrød
QUICK DANISH RYE BREAD

This is a quick no-sourdough-starter-ready sort of rye bread, so when I say 'quick'
I mean quicker than the 5 days needed for the traditional Danish rye bread. It's my
'oh no, I killed the sourdough again' recipe. It happens...

50 g/2 oz. kibbled/cracked
rye

25 g/$^7/_8$ oz. fresh yeast

300 ml/1$^1/_4$ cups buttermilk

2 tablespoons barley malt
syrup

500 g/scant 5 cups dark
rye flour

100 g/$^3/_4$ cup white strong
bread flour

1 teaspoon salt

50 g/$^3/_8$ cup flaxseeds/
linseeds

50 g/$^3/_8$ cup sunflower
seeds

**MAKES 1 LARGE
OR 2 SMALL LOAVES**

Place the kibbled/cracked rye in a saucepan with water to cover and
bring to the boil, then reduce the heat and simmer for 3–4 minutes.
Drain and set aside.

Place the yeast in the bowl of a stand mixer. Add 150 ml/$^2/_3$ cup
lukewarm water and stir until it starts to dissolve. Add the buttermilk,
then the barley malt syrup. Start adding the flours, salt, seeds and the
drained rye kernels. Knead for 5 minutes. If the dough feels too dry,
add a little water – or more flour if too wet. Cover and leave to rise for
at least 40 minutes in a nice warm place. You can let it rise for much
longer in a cooler place, too.

Knead the dough again and shape into one large loaf or two smaller
ones and place in lined loaf pans. Cover and leave to rise for at least
another 30 minutes.

Preheat the oven to 180°C (350°F) Gas 4.

Brush top of loaves with water and use a fork to prick holes all the
way along to stop the top cracking and rising unevenly. Bake in the
preheated oven for 1$^1/_4$ hours for a larger loaf and 40–45 minutes for
smaller ones – the loaves are done when internal temperature reaches
98°C/208°F. Turn out and cover with a damp tea towel/dish towel to
prevent a hard crust forming. Leave to cool completely before slicing.

julekake
NORWEGIAN CHRISTMAS BREAD

Every household in Norway has a recipe for *julekake*. Literally translated, it means 'Christmas cake', but as it's a dough with yeast, it's actually closer to a bread (some Norwegians do call it *julebrød*, or 'Christmas bread'). Throughout the festive season *julekake* is enjoyed warm or toasted, with lashings of butter and *brunost* (Norway's sweet brown whey cheese).

25 g/$^7/_8$ oz. fresh yeast

200 ml/$^3/_4$ cup whole milk, heated to 36–37°C/97–98°F (no hotter than this)

50 g/$^1/_4$ cup caster/superfine sugar

100 ml/$^1/_3$ cup soured milk (or other similar dairy product)

50 g/3$^1/_2$ tablespoons butter, softened

1 teaspoon salt

400–500 g/3–3$^1/_2$ cups white strong bread flour, plus extra for dusting

1 teaspoon ground cardamom

1 egg, beaten

oil, for brushing

pearl/nibbed sugar, for sprinkling (optional)

FILLING

50 g/$^3/_8$ cup raisins

freshly squeezed juice of 1 orange

50–75 g/$^3/_8$–$^2/_3$ cup chopped mixed peel (optional)

MAKES 1 LOAF

A few hours before you start to bake, soak the raisins for the filling in the orange juice.

Add the yeast and warm milk to the bowl of a stand mixer and stir to dissolve. Add the sugar and stir to dissolve a bit, then add the soured milk and soft butter. Add the salt to half of the flour and add this to the mixture along with the ground cardamom and mix until smooth.

Pour in the beaten egg, reserving some for brushing. Spoon in more flour if needed, until you have a smooth, kneaded dough that is still slightly sticky. Squeeze any excess juice from the raisins and add them to the dough. At this stage, you can add mixed peel if you like, depending on how fruity you like your loaf.

Brush the dough lightly with oil and cover it with clingfilm/plastic wrap. Leave it to rise until it has doubled in size (this should take about an hour or so, depending on how warm the kitchen is).

On a floured surface, turn out the dough and knead it to get the air out. Shape it into a round cob-loaf style and place on a baking sheet lined with baking parchment (you don't need a loaf pan). Leave the bread to rise for another 20–25 minutes, then brush it with the remaining egg.

Preheat the oven to around 170°C (340°F) Gas 3$^1/_2$.

Bake the bread in the preheated oven for around 40 minutes until baked through. If the loaf starts going a bit too dark during baking, cover it with foil. As soon as the bread is done, remove it from the oven and sprinkle pearl/nibbed sugar over the top if you wish, then cover with a damp tea towel/dish towel to prevent a hard crust forming while it cools.

grøvboller med frø
SEEDED ROLLS

Good for the *smörgåsbord*, good for packed lunches on a snowy hike, and good in the morning with a cup of coffee. You can change the seeds to suit whatever you have in the storecupboard.

100 g/³/₄ cup pumpkin seeds

100 g/³/₄ cup sunflower seeds

50 g/³/₈ cup flaxseeds/linseeds

100 g/1 cup chopped rye kernels/rye berries

25 g/⁷/₈ oz. fresh yeast

2 tablespoons barley malt syrup (or sugar)

250 ml/1 cup buttermilk (or other soured dairy culture)

4 tablespoons vegetable oil

200 g/2 cups dark rye flour (wholegrain)

500 g/3¹/₂ cups white strong bread flour

2 teaspoons salt

beaten egg, for brushing

MAKES 18

Set aside half the pumpkin seeds and half the sunflower seeds for the topping.

Place the remaining pumpkin seeds and sunflower seeds, all the flaxseeds/linseeds and all the rye kernels/berries in a saucepan with water to cover. Bring to the boil, then simmer for 3–4 minutes. Drain and set aside to cool.

In the bowl of a stand mixer, add the yeast and 100 ml/¹/₃ cup lukewarm water (no warmer than 37°C/98°F) and allow to dissolve for a few minutes, then add the syrup and buttermilk. (If you can't get barley malt syrup, use dark syrup or even granulated sugar.) Add the oil. Keep mixing and gradually add the flours and salt. You may not need all the flour, or you may need a little extra. Knead for about 5 minutes in the machine until the dough is stretchy. Cover the bowl and set aside in a warm place to rise for at least an hour. You can also let it rise in a cooler place for longer.

Knead the dough by hand, then roll to a 20 x 45-cm/8 x 18-in. rectangle. Brush gently with beaten egg, then scatter the reserved seeds over the top and press them lightly into the dough. Cut into 18 pieces, place on a baking sheet and leave to rise for another 30 minutes.

Preheat the oven to 180°C (350°F) Gas 4.

Bake the rolls in the preheated oven for around 14–15 minutes or until done. Remove from the oven and leave to cool slightly before serving.

juleboller
CHRISTMAS BUNS

I love a nice, sweet breakfast during the cold days of winter. These buns are a version of a recipe my grandmother used to make for my sisters and me on our birthdays. They're quite sweet, and are best eaten straight out of the oven with a lot of butter and a cup of hot chocolate or strong tea. At Christmas time, I add raisins or chocolate pieces, and spice up the buns with some ground cardamom.

100 ml/⅓ cup double/heavy cream

300 ml/1¼ cups whole milk

50 g/1¾ oz. fresh yeast

80 g/6½ tablespoons caster/superfine sugar

1 teaspoon ground cardamom

1 teaspoon salt

approx. 800 g/5¾ cups white strong bread flour, plus extra for dusting

1 egg

100 ml/⅓ cup Greek yogurt (or other soured dairy product)

150 g/⅔ cup butter, softened

100 g/¾ cup raisins or 100 g/⅔ cup chocolate chips (optional)

beaten egg, for brushing

pearl/nibbed sugar, to decorate (optional)

MAKES 24
(IF YOU WISH, HALVE THE RECIPE, OR FREEZE THE BAKED BUNS AFTER THEY'VE COOLED AND DEFROST AS NEEDED)

Attach the dough hook to your stand mixer. Heat the cream and milk until finger-warm (36–37°C/97–99°F), then break the yeast into the liquid. Stir until dissolved, then tip into the mixer bowl. Add the sugar and ground cardamom, then stir again. Add the salt to the flour, then start to spoon it into the bowl bit by bit until about half is used up. Next, add the egg, yogurt and softened butter as you keep mixing. Continue to add the rest of the flour – you might not need it all.

Keep mixing until you have a dough that is a bit sticky, but starting to let go of the sides of the bowl. This will take 5–7 minutes. The dough is ready to rise when it starts to let go of the sides of the bowl. If using, add the raisins or chocolate chips.

Cover the bowl with clingfilm/plastic wrap and leave in a warm place to rise for 35–40 minutes until doubled in size.

Turn the dough out onto a lightly floured surface, then knead with your hands, adding more flour if needed. Cut the dough into 24 equal pieces and roll them until uniformly round. Place on a baking sheet lined with baking parchment, cover again and leave to rise for a further 20 minutes.

Preheat the oven to 200°C (400°F) Gas 6.

Brush each bun lightly with egg, then sprinkle over pearl/nibbed sugar if using. Bake in the preheated oven for 10–12 minutes, or until baked through (this will vary depending on your oven).

Remove from the oven and cover with a damp tea towel/dish towel for 5 minutes if you prefer buns without a hard crust. Serve sliced and open with butter or Scandinavian cheese.

CAKES AND DESSERTS

Here are comforting bakes and dishes for the colder days when only a little sweetness will do. A treat to end the meal, or a fancy wreath cake for seeing in the New Year, or perhaps a spot of baking because friends are popping round for some cosy afternoon Christmas *hygge*.

crème brûlée med havtorn

SEA BUCKTHORN CRÈME BRÛLÉE

We have a family tradition of making crème brûlée on New Year's Eve, and tart berries such as the sea buckthorn can really lift a creamy dessert. Sea buckthorn grows all across Scandinavia, and in some sandy areas of England and Scotland, among other places. The orange berries are quite sour when raw but fabulous once cooked (try sea buckthorn jam or compote). Ideally, make these the day before serving them.

450 ml/scant 2 cups double/heavy cream

50 ml/3½ tablespoons milk

80 ml/5½ tablespoons pure sea buckthorn juice

50 g/¼ cup sugar

5 egg yolks

1 teaspoon vanilla sugar or extract (or vanilla pod/bean, if you prefer)

demerara/turbinado sugar, for the topping

sea buckthorn berries (optional)

high-sided roasting pan

4 large ramekins (or 5 smaller ones) that can fit easily inside the pan

cook's thermometer

cook's blowtorch

MAKES 4 GENEROUS DESSERTS (OR 5 SMALLER ONES)

Preheat the oven to 140°C (275°F) Gas 1. Boil a full kettle of water.

In a saucepan, add the cream, milk and sea buckthorn juice and start to heat up.

In a bowl, whisk the sugar, egg yolks and vanilla (if using a pod/bean, add it to the saucepan instead) until the mixture turns a lighter colour.

Bring the cream mixture to boiling point (don't whisk it, just stir), then take off the heat. Pour a small amount of the hot cream into the egg mixture while stirring. Make sure it is incorporated, then repeat a few times with just a dash of the hot cream each time. This is to ensure the egg does not scramble.

Pour the egg mixture into the pan of cream and gently whisk together. Try not to create any air bubbles, as these will end up on top of each crème brûlée, spoiling the smooth surface. Pour the crème into the ramekins and place in the roasting pan. Carefully pour the hot water into the roasting pan until the ramekin sides are covered to at least a depth of 1.5 cm/⅝ in. Be careful not to splash any of the crèmes. Cover the roasting pan with foil and make a few air holes.

Bake in the preheated oven until set – depending on your ramekins, this should take around 25–30 minutes. Use a cook's thermometer to check that the internal temperature of the crèmes has reached 77–79°C (170–174°F).

Carefully remove the roasting pan from the oven, extract the ramekins and leave for 20 minutes to cool down. Once cooled, transfer to the fridge until the next day.

Before serving, add a generous spoonful of demerara/turbinado sugar to the top of the crèmes, then, using a cook's blowtorch, grill the tops until they're melted and a caramelized crust has formed. If you can get hold of some sea buckthorn berries, make a compote with berries and sugar and add it to the top of the dishes as decoration.

marengskrans
MERINGUE WREATH

One Christmas I had guests who didn't like rice pudding (see page 152), so I made this instead, as it also uses the Danish cherry sauce I would have made for the *risalamande*. It's not traditionally Scandinavian, but it is so indulgent and beautiful that I just had to include it here as it's a great alternative to rice pudding and it has the same flavours. Add the filling just before serving to prevent the meringue going soggy.

PAVLOVA MERINGUE BASE

4 egg whites

125 g/^{7}/$_8$ cup icing/ confectioners' sugar

1 teaspoon white wine vinegar

1 teaspoon vanilla sugar or extract

1^1/$_2$ teaspoons cornflour/ cornstarch

FILLING

200 ml/1 cup whipping cream

150 ml/^{2}/$_3$ cup Pastry Cream (see page 136)

50 ml/3^1/$_2$ tablespoons pistachio liqueur (I use Serravinci Pistacchino)

1 quantity of Danish Cherry Sauce (see page 152), or use a ready-made cherry sauce or fruit filling (adding a dash of lemon juice to take off the sweetness and a dash of water if it's too thick)

50 g/^{1}/$_2$ cup chopped, toasted pistachio nuts

2 piping/pastry bags

SERVES 6–8

Preheat the oven to 200°C (400°F) Gas 6.

To make the meringue, whisk the egg whites to soft peaks in a very clean bowl. Add the icing/confectioners' sugar one spoon at a time, whisking continuously – do not stop whisking! Whisk for about 5 minutes, or until you have a very stiff mixture. Stir in the vinegar and vanilla. Add the cornflour/cornstarch and fold in.

On a piece of baking parchment, use a pencil to lightly draw a circle of around 20-cm/8-in. diameter, then a circle inside that, around 10-cm/4-in. diameter. Place the parchment on a baking sheet.

Spoon the meringue into a piping/pastry bag and cut a large opening at the end – be quick and careful doing this. Pipe into a circle on the parchment using the pencil lines as a rough guide. It doesn't need to be exact, you just need to end up with a uniform circle. Form a slight trench around the middle of the meringue circle, around 2 cm/^{3}/$_4$ in. wide and 1 cm/^{1}/$_2$ in. deep. This will help to keep the filling in place.

Turn the oven down to 120°C (250°F) Gas ^{1}/$_2$. Place the meringue on the lowest shelf and bake for 1 hour, maybe even a little longer. The meringue is done when it looks pale and dry, but the middle bit is still sticky (carefully insert a skewer to check). Turn off the oven and leave the meringue inside with the door ajar for at least a few hours, or overnight if possible.

To make the filling, whip the cream to form soft peaks, then fold in the pastry cream, followed by the pistachio liqueur. Spoon the cream into a piping/pastry bag, snip off the end and use the trench on the meringue to guide you as you pipe the cream on.

Drizzle over as much cold cherry sauce as you like, but don't go overboard – serve the rest in a bowl for people to help themselves. Sprinkle the toasted pistachios over the top and serve immediately.

medaljer
GINGER BISCUIT MEDALS

In Denmark there is a popular afternoon coffee treat known as *medaljer*, which means 'medals' (probably due to their appearance!). They are usually made with shortcrust sweet pastry, but I once made them using leftover ginger biscuit/cookie dough and they were a big hit at home.

½ quantity of Swedish Ginger Biscuits dough (see page 53)

150 g/1 cup icing/confectioners' sugar, plus 1 tablespoon

200 ml/¾ cup whipping cream

½ teaspoon vanilla sugar or extract

½ quantity of Pastry Cream (see below) – alternatively use store-bought

plain/all-purpose flour, for dusting

red berries, such as raspberries or redcurrants, to decorate

PASTRY CREAM

1 egg yolk

50 g/¼ cup caster/superfine sugar

1 tablespoon cornflour/cornstarch

250 ml/1 cup whole milk

seeds from ½ vanilla pod/bean

15 g/1 tablespoon butter

a pinch of salt

a round cookie cutter approx. 6–7 cm/2½ –2¾ in. in diameter

2 piping/pastry bags

MAKES 6

Preheat the oven to 200°C (400°F) Gas 6. Line two baking sheets with baking parchment.

Dust your work surface with flour and roll out the dough to a thickness of approx. 2 mm/⅛ in. Using the cookie cutter, cut out 16 circles (you only need 12, but some bake unevenly so cut extra). Place on the lined baking sheets. Bake in the preheated oven for 6–7 minutes until baked through – oven times can vary, so keep an eye on them. Leave to cool and crisp up.

Mix the icing/confectioners' sugar with drops of hot water to make a thick but smooth mixture – it needs to be pipe-able, but too thin and it will flood; too thick and it will be difficult to pipe. Put in a piping/pastry bag and cut a small opening. Place six baked rounds on the work surface, pipe the icing in a neat circle on the biscuits and let dry.

Whip the cream with the vanilla sugar and the extra tablespoon of icing/confectioners' sugar until stiff, then place in a piping/pastry bag fitted with a star nozzle/tip. Place the remaining six rounds on a plate and spoon 1 tablespoon of pastry cream (see below) on each one, then pipe on whipped cream to a height of 2.5 cm/1 in. Carefully place the iced tops on the cream. Add more whipped cream and berries to decorate.

Pastry cream

Makes approx. 300 g/10½ oz. so you may have some left over (use within 2–3 days in cakes or pastries, or in the meringue wreath on page 135). If using this recipe for a standard layer cake, double it but use 1 egg yolk and 1 whole egg.

In a bowl, whisk together the egg yolk, sugar and cornflour/cornstarch.

Place the milk in a pan with the vanilla seeds, bring to the boil, then take the pan off the heat and pour one-third into the egg mixture while whisking. Once whisked, pour back into the pan and bring back to the boil, whisking continuously. Let it thicken for a minute, making sure it does not burn, then remove from the heat and stir in the butter and salt. Pour into a bowl and leave to cool (place baking parchment on top to stop a skin forming). Use only when cold.

chokladrulltårta
EASY CHOCOLATE ROLL

Sometimes simple things work the best. I often make this with the kids and simply amend the fillings according to what I have in the cupboard. There are times when I add fruit and berries, other times more chocolate. When we make this roll for Christmas, we turn it into a log and go overboard with the chocolate decorations.

You can also replace the cocoa with equal quantities of plain/all-purpose flour to make a vanilla roll instead – this recipe is versatile.

4 eggs

120 g/²/₃ cup minus 1 tablespoon caster/superfine sugar

90 g/²/₃ cup plain/all-purpose flour

30 g/¹/₃ cup cocoa powder, plus extra for dusting

¹/₂ teaspoon baking powder

a pinch of salt

1 teaspoon vanilla sugar or extract

25 g/1³/₄ tablespoons butter, melted and cooled

50 g/2 oz. dark/bittersweet chocolate, roughly chopped, for the topping

FILLING

300 ml/1¹/₄ cups whipping cream

brandy or walnut liqueur (optional)

75 g/³/₄ cup toasted, chopped walnut pieces

Swiss roll/jelly roll pan, approx. 30 x 20 cm/12 x 8 in.

SERVES 6–7

Preheat the oven to 180°C (350°F) Gas 4. Line the Swiss roll/jelly roll pan with baking parchment and non-stick spray.

In the bowl of a stand mixer, add the eggs and the sugar and whisk until they reach the ribbon stage (this may take several minutes on full speed). It's done when you can see ribbon traces on the surface when lifting the whisk from the bowl.

Mix the flour, cocoa powder, baking powder, salt and vanilla together, then sieve into the egg mixture and fold gently until combined. Add the melted butter and fold in, being careful not to knock the air out.

Pour the mixture into the prepared pan. Bake in the preheated oven until just baked through – the time will depend on your oven, but it is around 10–12 minutes. It is done when it is slightly springy to the touch.

Remove from the oven and allow to cool for a few minutes. Cover the pan with a clean tea towel/dish towel, then turn the cake out onto the tea towel/dish towel. Carefully remove the paper backing. Gently roll the log around the tea towel/dish towel while it is still warm – this should prevent the roll from cracking later when filled. Leave to cool.

Meanwhile, for the filling, whip the cream to form stiff peaks. When the roll has cooled, unroll carefully and brush with the brandy or walnut liqueur, if using. Add the whipped cream in a thin, even layer and top with the chopped walnuts. Carefully roll it back around the cream and place on a serving tray.

Dust the roll with cocoa powder. Melt the chocolate in a bain-marie or microwave. Add to a piping/pastry bag and snip the end off, then pipe the chocolate all across the roll and serve.

julecrumble
CHRISTMAS CRUMBLE

I love a crumble. They're fuss-free and taste even better on the second day, if there's any left! An apple crumble is a British classic, but I've introduced a couple of elements from Denmark for a twist. The marzipan is decadent, but it is Christmas after all.

6-7 sharp apples (such as Granny Smith)

1 teaspoon good-quality vanilla paste (or the seeds from 1 vanilla pod/bean)

100 g/3^1/2 oz. frozen lingonberries

TOPPING

100 g/^{1}/2 cup soft light brown sugar

100 g/7 tablespoons butter

100 g/1 cup ground almonds

100 g/^{3}/4 cup plain/all-purpose flour

1 teaspoon ground cinnamon

a pinch of ground cardamom

a pinch of salt

50 g/2 oz. marzipan (minimum 50% almonds), grated

flaked/slivered almonds, to taste

SERVES 4-5

Preheat the oven to 180°C (350°F) Gas 4.

Peel the apples, core and chop into bite-sized pieces. Place in a saucepan with the vanilla and a dash of water, then stew slightly over a medium heat until starting to soften.

For the topping, place the sugar, butter, ground almonds, flour, spices and salt in a food processor (or do it by hand) and mix until it starts to crumble, but is clumping together slightly.

Add the apples to an ovenproof dish and top with the lingonberries. Tip over the crumble. Scatter over the grated marzipan and flaked/slivered almonds, then bake in the preheated oven for 25–30 minutes until crispy and the apple mixture has cooked through.

Serve with vanilla ice cream or custard.

saffranstårta

SAFFRON LAYER CAKE

Saffron is one of the most festive spices in Scandinavia, especially in Sweden, so I sometimes use it in a cake. It has the flavours of our Christmas, but is a bit fancier than serving a saffron bun. Grind your own saffron in a pestle and mortar if you cannot get hold of ground saffron. If you are not a fan of marzipan, you can omit it from the buttercream filling and simply add some apple or pear compote between the layers for extra flavour.

50 g/3½ tablespoons butter

100 ml/⅓ cup milk

0.5 g/a small pinch of ground saffron

4 eggs

325 g/1⅝ cups caster/superfine sugar

300 g/2¼ cups plain/all-purpose flour

2 teaspoons baking powder

1 teaspoon vanilla sugar or extract

½ teaspoon salt

50 g/¼ cup Greek yogurt or similar

frosted redcurrants, to decorate (optional)

MARZIPAN BUTTERCREAM

75 g/2¾ oz. marzipan (at least 50% almonds), grated

300 g/2 cups plus 2 tablespoons icing/confectioners' sugar

150 g/⅔ cup butter, softened

a few tablespoons of milk (optional)

freshly squeezed lemon juice (optional)

3 x 18-cm/7-in. round cake pans

SERVES 6–8

Preheat the oven to 180°C (350°F) Gas 4. Grease and line three 18-cm/7-in. diameter round cake pans. You can use larger cake pans, but your cake will be wider and not as tall.

Melt the butter in a saucepan, then add the milk and saffron and set aside to infuse.

Whisk the eggs and sugar together until thick and fluffy. Mix the dry ingredients together, then sift into the sugar mixture and fold in. Add the yogurt and the saffron milk to the mixture and fold again until incorporated.

Pour the batter into the prepared pans, dividing it evenly, and bake in the preheated oven for around 12–14 minutes or until a skewer inserted into the centre comes out clean. Saffron is quite drying, so take care not to over-bake. Every oven varies, so keep an eye on the cakes.

Leave the layers to cool in the pans while you make the buttercream. Add a few tablespoons of boiling water to the marzipan and mix it with a fork to melt it slightly (this avoids lumps of marzipan in the buttercream). Using an electric beater, in a bowl mix the sugar and butter on high speed and add the marzipan. You may need to add a bit of milk, too. Beat and allow to fluff up for several minutes on high speed. If you feel it is too sweet, you can add a few drops of lemon juice or similar.

Remove the cakes from the pans and peel off the paper. Place the first layer of cake on the serving plate, then add a layer of the buttercream. Repeat until you have used all three layers. You can leave the cake naked and just decorate the top with the remaining buttercream or you can use the buttercream to give a light coating all around the sides, as shown here, for a very frosty-looking cake. I like to decorate it with frosted redcurrants for that festive snowy look.

multekrem

CLOUDBERRY CREAM

This recipe simply had to be included in this book, because it is such a huge part of Christmas in Norway. It's very traditional, but also very simple. Cloudberries only grow wild near the Arctic Circle and have a short season of just a few weeks in July and August. They are hard to cultivate and hard to pick (the plump orange berries tend to burst in your hand), which makes them highly sought-after and quite pricey (unless you are lucky enough to know someone who knows where they grow). In the US and Canada, the cloudberry is also referred to as a 'bakeapple' (*rubus chamaemorus*).

In Norway, *multekrem* is sometimes served with *krumkaker*, which are thin, crispy conicle waffles, but you rarely find them elsewhere. Cloudberry cream also goes very well with crêpes, so if you want to serve this with something, then whip up a batch and serve alongside.

2 tablespoons brown or caster/superfine sugar

250 g/9 oz. cloudberries (frozen berries can be used, or use cloudberry jam if berries aren't available – if using jam, you won't need to add any sugar)

300 ml/1^1/$_2$ cups whipping cream

1 teaspoon vanilla extract or vanilla sugar

SERVES 4

Scatter the sugar over the berries and allow it to soak in (save any juice that drains off).

Whip the cream with the vanilla until stiff. Reserving a few berries for decoration, carefully fold the cloudberries and cream together, then spoon into individual serving glasses.

Any leftover juice can be added on top just before serving, along with the reserved berries.

honningkage
HONEY LAYER CAKE

One of my most favourite cakes ever! The baker in my village sold this in winter and I'd buy a slice to eat on the way home from school. Use three round cake pans – I use 18-cm/7-in. ones, but you can use slightly larger ones and the cake will simply be shorter, but wider (do keep an eye on the baking time).

125 ml/^{3}/$_8$ cup runny honey

80 ml/^{1}/$_4$ cup golden/corn syrup

50 g/^{1}/$_4$ cup caster/superfine sugar

2 whole eggs and 2 egg yolks

300 g/2^1/$_4$ cups plain/all-purpose flour

1^1/$_2$ teaspoons bicarbonate of/baking soda

^{1}/$_2$ teaspoon baking powder

a pinch of salt

2 teaspoons ground cinnamon

1 teaspoon ground cardamom

1 teaspoon ground ginger

1 teaspoon ground cloves

grated zest from 1 orange

250 ml/1 cup buttermilk

150 ml/^{2}/$_3$ cup double/heavy cream

BUTTERCREAM FILLING

100 g/^{1}/$_2$ cup caster/superfine sugar

125 g/9 tablespoons butter, softened

1 egg yolk

1 teaspoon vanilla sugar, or seeds from ^{1}/$_2$ vanilla pod/bean

CHOCOLATE GLAZE

40 g/3 tablespoons butter

100 g/3^1/$_2$ oz. dark/bittrsweet chocolate

2 tablespoons golden/corn syrup

chocolate sprinkles

SERVES 6-8

Preheat the oven to 170°C (340°F) Gas 3^1/$_2$. Line the three cake pans with baking parchment – see above for pan sizes.

Over a low heat, combine the honey, golden/corn syrup and sugar with 100 ml/^{1}/$_3$ cup water in a saucepan until melted together. Leave to cool until tepid.

Add the eggs (both whole and yolks) to the bowl of a stand mixer and whisk to combine. Slowly add the tepid syrup mixture into the eggs, beating continuously on high speed.

Combine the flour, bicarbonate of/baking soda, baking powder, salt and spices together, then fold into the egg mixture. Add the orange zest, buttermilk and cream and fold until smooth.

Pour one-third of the batter into each prepared cake pan. Bake in the preheated oven for around 8–10 minutes, or until well risen, golden brown and springy to the touch. A skewer inserted into the middle should come out clean. Leave to cool for a few minutes in the pans, then turn out onto a wire rack and allow to cool completely.

To make the buttercream, make a sugar syrup by gently heating the sugar in a pan with 2 tablespoons water until fully dissolved. Leave to cool a little. Whisk the butter, egg yolk and vanilla together on high speed, then slowly add the sugar syrup, whisking well with each addition. Continue beating for several minutes until creamy and fluffy. If it does not go fluffy, pop the mixture in the fridge for 30 minutes, then whip again when slightly cooled (if the butter is too soft, or the sugar too hot, it may not whip properly at first, but it will be fine when a bit colder).

To assemble, place one cake layer on a serving plate, cover generously with half the fluffy buttercream, then repeat with the other layers.

To make the chocolate glaze, melt the butter, chocolate and syrup in a heatproof bowl set over a pan of hot water. Let it cool ever so slightly. Spread over the top of the cake, scatter over chocolate sprinkles and leave the topping to harden before serving.

æbletrifli
APPLE TRIFLE

This is a pimped-up version of a very traditional Norwegian and Danish dessert known as either *tilslørte bondepiker* or *æblekage* – layers of crispy breadcrumbs, apple compote and thick cream – utterly delicious, but more of an everyday dessert. Here, I've added a cake layer to make it more like a trifle, but have kept the crunch by adding some hazelnuts and oats.

APPLE COMPOTE
1 kg/2 lb. 4 oz. tart apples (Bramleys or Granny Smiths)

1 vanilla pod/bean, seeds scraped out, or vanilla extract

3 tablespoons sugar

CAKE LAYER
125 g/1 cup minus 1 tablespoon plain/all-purpose flour

$^1/_2$ teaspoon bicarbonate of/baking soda

a pinch of salt

1 teaspoon ground cinnamon

1 teaspoon mixed spice/apple pie spice

75 g/$^1/_3$ cup softened butter

100 g/$^1/_2$ cup caster/superfine sugar

1 egg

HAZELNUT-OAT CRUNCH
50 g/3$^1/_2$ tablespoons butter

40 g/3$^1/_4$ tablespoons golden caster/superfine sugar

25 g/$^1/_4$ cup rolled/old-fashioned oats

50 g/1 cup panko breadcrumbs

50 g/$^1/_4$ cup chopped hazelnuts

TO ASSEMBLE THE TRIFLE
150 ml/$^2/_3$ cup good-quality cold custard

200 ml/$^3/_4$ cup whipped cream (forming soft peaks)

SERVES 6–8

To make the compote, peel, core and chop the apples. Place in a pan with the vanilla, sugar and 100 ml/$^1/_3$ cup water and bring to the boil. Simmer for about 20 minutes until the apples are mushy, then leave to cool. Remove the vanilla pod/bean, if using. The compote needs to be quite tart to balance the cake and cream. This makes enough for the cake base and trifle.

To make the cake layer, you will need a 20 x 20-cm/8 x 8-in. cake pan, or the equivalent (it needs to be a relatively thin layer). Preheat the oven to 170°C (340°F) Gas 3$^1/_2$.

Combine the flour, bicarbonate of/baking soda, salt, cinnamon and mixed spice/apple pie spice in a bowl, and set aside. Beat the butter and sugar until fluffy, then add the egg and keep beating until incorporated. Fold in the dry ingredients, followed by 150 g/5$^1/_2$ oz. of the apple compote. Once combined, pour the mixture into the cake pan and bake in the preheated oven for around 10 minutes until just baked through. Insert a skewer into the centre – if it comes out clean, it's done. This is a thin layer, so it won't take long. Leave to cool.

To make the hazelnut-oat crunch, melt the butter in a frying pan/skillet, then add the sugar and stir until melted. Add the oats and breadcrumbs and fry for several minutes, allowing them to crisp up. Add the nuts and fry for a few more minutes – be careful not to over-toast the nuts, as they can go bitter. Once everything is crispy, turn out into a bowl and leave to cool, stirring once in a while to break up any lumps.

To assemble the trifle, put a layer of the remaining apple compote in a glass trifle bowl as the base, then add a layer of the cake. Add more compote, followed by a good layer of the crunch, then apple again. Add a layer of custard, followed by crunch, then apple, then cake. Repeat again, reserving a bit of the crunch to decorate. Finally, spread the whipped cream on top. Leave to set in the fridge for at least an hour. Just before serving, add the rest of the crunch on the top to decorate.

risengrød
RICE PUDDING

At Christmas, rice pudding (we actually call it 'rice porridge') is a big deal all over Scandinavia. We eat warm, unsweetened rice pudding with cinnamon, sugar and a knob of butter, and on Christmas Eve we serve the cold pudding with a few additions (see page 152). Scandinavians always make rice pudding on the hob/stovetop, never in the oven, and we don't sweeten it because the toppings are sweet. This recipe makes enough for rice pudding for 23rd December as well as dessert on Christmas Eve. If you only want to serve one of the two dishes, reduce the recipe by half.

It's said that Scandinavian Christmas elves love rice pudding, so we always leave out a bowl for them as a thank-you for taking care of the house, farm and animals throughout the year. If you forget to do this, they will play tricks on you in the coming year!

400 g/2 cups pudding rice
2 litres/2 quarts whole milk
1 whole vanilla pod/bean
salt, sugar and/or vanilla extract, if needed
butter and cinnamon sugar, to serve

SERVES 4 (WITH ENOUGH LEFTOVER TO MAKE THE DESSERT ON PAGE 152)

In a heavy-based saucepan, add the rice and 600 ml/2$\frac{1}{2}$ cups water and bring to the boil for a good few minutes, then add all the milk and the vanilla pod/bean. Bring to the boil for around 5 minutes, stirring constantly to avoid the rice sticking to the bottom of the saucepan. Turn the heat down to low, cover and simmer, stirring occasionally, until the rice is cooked through but not overcooked (around 25–35 minutes – do check). It's important to keep a close eye on the pan as it can burn or boil over.

Once cooked, add a little salt to taste (never add the salt until the rice has cooked through). You can add a little sugar if you prefer a sweeter pudding or a few drops of vanilla extract.

The pudding may still be a little liquid when the rice is cooked. Don't worry as the milk will soak into the rice as it cools if using with the dessert. If you are keeping half of the rice pudding for the dessert on page 152 and eating the other half immediately, reserve half in the fridge for the dessert and simply boil the rest with no lid for a little while longer until the rice pudding is thicker. Remove the vanilla pod/bean once cooked and discard.

Serve the hot rice pudding in bowls topped with a knob of butter in the middle and a generous amount of cinnamon sugar sprinkled over (mix one part ground cinnamon with three parts granulated or caster/superfine sugar).

Tip: If you are trying to reduce the fat in your food, you can use skimmed milk instead. The result is less creamy, but still delicious.

risalamande/ris à la malta/riskrem
CHRISTMAS RICE PUDDING

'A loved child has many names' is a Scandinavian saying that is apt for this dish – Danes adopted a French name meaning 'almond rice', while it seems Swedes misunderstood Danish pronunciation and called it 'Maltese rice'. Norwegians rightly just call it 'rice cream'.

50 g/⅜ cup blanched almonds

250 ml/1 cup whipping/heavy cream

2 tablespoons icing/confectioners' sugar

1 teaspoon vanilla sugar or extract

½ quantity of Rice Pudding (see page 151), chilled

SERVES 6

Roughly chop the almonds, except for one which must be kept whole.

Whip the cream with the sugar and vanilla until thick, then gently fold it into the chilled rice pudding. If the rice pudding is too cold and hard to fold, leave it out at room temperature for a while. Add the almonds, including the reserved whole one, and pour into your serving dish. Pop it back in the fridge until ready to serve with one of the sauces below.

Some people prefer a very creamy version, and some less so - you can vary the quantity of cream accordingly. The rice is served cold, while the sauce is hot.

apelsinsås
SWEDISH ORANGE SAUCE

2–3 tablespoons orange juice

75 g/6 tablespoons sugar

2 oranges, peeled, pith and pips removed

When making the rice pudding, add 2–3 tablespoons orange juice to the whipped cream before folding into the rice. In a pan, bring the sugar and 100 ml/7 tablespoons water to the boil until the sugar is dissolved, then take off the heat. Slice the oranges 5-mm/¼ -in. thick, add to the warm sugar syrup. Add a few slices to top the *ris à la malta*.

rød saus
NORWEGIAN RED SAUCE

250 g/2 cups frozen berries (raspberries or strawberries are good)

50–100 g/¼–½ cup sugar, to taste

freshly squeezed lemon juice (optional)

Place the frozen berries in a pan with 100 ml/7 tablespoons water and sugar to taste. Bring to the boil, then simmer to let the berries break up. Whizz it with a stick blender until smooth. If it needs a little something, add a few drops of lemon juice before serving with the *riskrem*.

kirsebærsovs
DANISH CHERRY SAUCE

1 heaped tablespoon cornflour/cornstarch (or arrowroot, as this prevents it going cloudly)

2 x 300-g/10½-oz. cans of black or morello cherries in syrup

1 teaspoon orange juice

2 tablespoons rum

Mix the cornflour/cornstarch with a small amount of syrup to make a paste. Bring the cherries and 250 ml/1 cup syrup to the boil in a pan, add the paste and stir. Boil for 1 minute to thicken, then take off the heat and add the orange juice and rum. Sweeten with sugar, if needed. Serve hot over cold *risalamande*.

kransekage /kransekake

ALMOND RING CAKE

Like many places, New Year's Eve in Scandinavia is all about fireworks and toasting the year ahead, but there are some traditions peculiar to the region. For example, in Denmark, people stand on chairs just before midnight and as the clock strikes, they jump off straight into the new year. Another, safer, tradition is the eating of this cake, known as *kransekage* in Denmark and *kranskake* in Norway. Made up of circles of marzipan that decrease in size from the bottom up, it is often served at midnight with a glass of champagne. It's so rich that you don't need much at all.

It's easiest to use special *kransekage* cake pans to make this cake (available online). The pans are rarely non-stick, so always use cake-release spray. If making the rings without using cake pans, check my blog at bronteaurell.com for measurements.

FOR A 10-RING KRANSEKAGE

100 g/3½ oz. egg whites

100 g/1 cup ground almonds

100 g/¾ cup icing/confectioners' sugar, plus extra for kneading

100 g/½ cup caster/superfine sugar

500 g/1 lb. 2 oz. marzipan (containing at least 60% almonds – if you can only find 50%, add more ground almonds)

1 teaspoon almond extract

ICING

½–1 small egg white

100 g/¾ cup icing/confectioners' sugar, plus extra as needed

kransekage cake pans (widely available online)

piping/pastry bag with a size 2 nozzle/tip

SERVES 15

To make the rings, in a bowl lightly whisk the egg whites until they're foaming. Add the ground almonds and both sugars, then whisk again until you have a smooth liquid paste. Grate the marzipan coarsely or break it into small pieces, and mix with the liquid. Your final dough will be sticky, but you will be able to handle it without getting too messy.

Put the dough in a plastic bag and chill in the fridge for at least 1 hour before using.

Preheat the oven to 200°C (400°F) Gas 6.

Cut a piece of the dough and work it with as much icing/confectioners' sugar as needed to make it rollable. Roll out your first piece (add more icing/confectioners' sugar if the dough is too sticky, or your ring looks like it might crack during baking). The most important thing is that all your rolls have to be smooth and exactly the same width and height – use a ruler if you want to be sure. If you rush this part of the process, the result will be a wonky tower. Take your time and repeat anything if unsure. Keep a glass of water to hand, as wet fingers can smooth out any inconsistencies and bumps. Starting with the smallest pan in the set and working your way outwards, make 10 perfectly-sized rings. The diameters of your rolls should be around 1–1.25 cm/½–⅝ in. There should be a little bit of dough left over, so use it to make a freehand top for your tower and place on a piece of baking parchment.

Continued overleaf

Continued from previous page

Place the pans on a baking sheet (never directly onto the oven shelf) and bake one layer at a time in the middle of the oven. They will need around 10–12 minutes until slightly golden brown.

Remove from the oven and allow to cool and dry before carefully removing from the pans.

To assemble the cake, first make the icing. Mix the egg white with the icing/confectioners' sugar, adding more sugar as needed. The icing needs to hold its shape, but still be light enough to comfortably pipe through a small, size-2 piping nozzle/tip. If the icing moves after piping, the cake will look messy. If you don't have a nozzle/tip, use a strong, good-quality piping/pastry bag and cut a small hole off the end.

It is most important that the outsides of the rings look good, as the insides will be hidden until eating. Starting with the bottom ring, carefully start the flow of the icing from inside and out, just enough so that the side of the ring is covered and then you immediately pull the icing back onto the other side in one continuous movement, back and forth. This is not a zig-zag pattern, it's more of a tight 'radio wave'. If you need to stop at any point to adjust the nozzle, do so when piping is at the top inner edge of the ring. Try to make sure the lines of icing are reasonably close together.

The icing can take a long time, but it is absolutely worth taking the time to do it right. After icing all the layers separately, you're ready to build the tower. Pipe a small trace of icing on the bottom ring, where it'll be covered by the one on top. Place that next one on top, and repeat until complete.

Traditional decorations for the *kranskage* are toothpick flags, or even streamers and mini Christmas crackers.

Tip: You can freeze the rings for up to 3 months. The cake also keeps at room temperature for several days, so you can make it ahead.

INDEX

ACKNOWLEDGEMENTS

'*Hele verden er en række af underværker... men vi er så vante til dem, at vi kalder dem hverdagsting.*'

'The whole world is a series of miracles... but we're so used to them we call them ordinary things.'

Hans Christian Andersen

Tak

Jonas, Astrid and Elsa: you make my Christmas real. I love you guys.

Thank you to the team at RPS who have worked so hard on this book: Cindy Richards, Julia Charles, Leslie Harrington, Sonya Nathoo, Pete Cassidy, Gillian Haslam, Tony Hutchinson, Kathy Kordalis (helped by Anna Hiddleston, Evangeline Harbury, Rebecca Spooner and Lizzie Wedderburn) and Patricia Harrington.

David Jørgensen, the most Christmas-loving person I know. Your joyful excitement at juletide brings me such pleasure! Also thank you for being my bestie, and for your red pen that always catches me out when it matters most.

My agents Jane Graham Maw and Vivienne Clore, for keeping me on the straight and narrow.

The huge clans that are the Blomhøjs and Aurells, and Ginny Clowes, who always ends up taste-testing recipes when she pops over. Live Sørdal and Martina Wade (and their mothers in Norway) for helping with Norwegian things. Rebekka Barnung and the rest of the fantastic ScandiKitchen team. Phil Thoms, David Holberton and David Cross for suggesting it would 'probably be a good idea' to write a Christmas book! To Jon Anders Fjelsrud for aquavit tips, and Sandi Toksvig for her support and encouragement, always.

Writing all my food books has never been a one-person job. Behind the scenes, scores of amazing people have helped out over the years, from everyone who has worked at ScandiKitchen over the years to the people who come to see us at the café every day and drink our coffee. To all our thousands of social media followers across the world, the Scandinavian community in the UK, and so many other fabulous people. There isn't enough space to thank you all, but you know who you are and this book is for you, with lots of Christmas love.

Also, thank you to Michael Bublé for making *the* Christmas album.

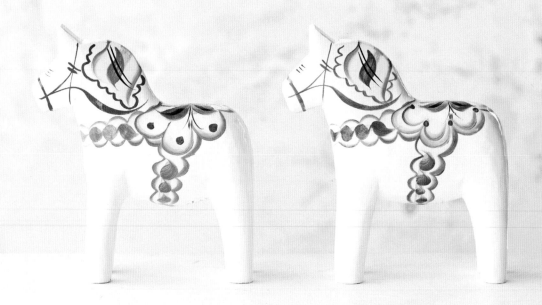